The Emotionally
Authentic Christian

The Emotionally Authentic Christian

✦

Building Passion, Creativity and Wholeness into Your Christian Walk

Bob Kalka

with foreword by Gary Gemmill, PhD

iUniverse, Inc.

New York Lincoln Shanghai

The Emotionally Authentic Christian
Building Passion, Creativity and Wholeness into Your Christian Walk

iUniverse books may be ordered through booksellers or by contacting:

iUniverse
2021 Pine Lake Road, Suite 100
Lincoln, NE 68512
www.iuniverse.com
1-800-Authors (1-800-288-4677)

ISBN: 978-0-595-42043-8 (pbk)
ISBN: 978-0-595-86388-4 (ebk)

Printed in the United States of America

Dedicated to all who have lost hope
for a time along their journey ...

and to those who are still searching.

Contents

Acknowledgments

No manuscript is ever the product of just its author, and that is certainly the case here. I am indebted to many special people for bringing this project to fruition, none more so than Dr. Gary Gemmill, my professional mentor for the past sixteen years, and Kelly Porter Kalka, my wife of almost that long, who has patiently experienced and learned many of the insights shared in these pages.

In addition, my sincerest thanks go out to the incredibly gifted Christians who substantially enhanced this work through their insightful reviews:

- Dr. William B. Lawrence, Dean of Perkins School of Theology at Southern Methodist University in Dallas, Texas

- Dr. Dan Bonner, President, the Center for Urban Congregational Renewal; United Methodist Elder; and Vice President for Development at Wesleyan Homes in Georgetown, Texas

- Claire Short, a gifted and accomplished therapist and author from Staines, Middlesex, in the United Kingdom

- Jacqueline Messer, a fellow leader of this research effort, from Round Rock, Texas.

Finally, I'd like to thank those others who have most encouraged and inspired me to pursue this work, either directly or indirectly—my dear children, Jonathan and Lauren; my parents, Bob Sr. and Joan Kalka; Rev. Doug and Marilyn Akers; Rev. Eric McKinney and Rev. Brenda Adkins of First United Methodist Church in Georgetown, Texas; Rev. Susan Gordon of Soul's Outreach Ministry in Austin, Texas; Rev. Stan Short from Staines Congregational Church in the United Kingdom; Dr. Crawford Loritts, Senior Pastor of Fellowship Bible Church in Roswell, Georgia; Mike Brewer, my friend and artist who developed the wonderful illustrations in this book; Bev Larkham; Tim Kalka; James Messer; Linda Valette; the staff and volunteers at Promise Keepers and RBC Ministries; and everyone else who has been touched through this work.

May God bless each of you every single day.

Foreword

Many of our churches are in a silent crisis today.

Are our congregations vibrant, filled with united and excited people creatively sharing their unique gifts with each other?

Or could many be better described as simply polite, largely populated with well-meaning yet somewhat detached groups and observers, with creativity something to be saved for another day?

Many of us Christians share this same crisis as individuals. How would you describe your own worship experience?

This book provides a powerful framework for practicing Christians to find a meaningful way to enliven not just their talk about Christ, but also their walk with him. It is about learning how to connect emotionally, spiritually, and intellectually with yourself more authentically, and how to carry this back into your congregational and daily living.

I have known the author since he was a graduate student in my classes on interpersonal and group dynamics many years ago, and I can remember well his excitement at discovering the power of experiential learning in the context of a group. Through committing himself to further intense experiences and research, he discovered a path of growth and understanding he had been searching for, which has culminated in his writing this book.

When I first began working with experiential learning groups, I also felt that I had finally found a meaningful, Spirit-led way to live my life on a daily basis. Prior to doing such groups, I puzzled over how I was to enact such spiritual directives as "love one another as I loved you." I knew that "love is the fulfilling of the law," but how was I to put this into practice on a daily basis?

To my delight, I found an authentic experience of the practice of Christianity within my early encounters with these groups, namely, (1) the confessing of faults, (2) the sharing of burdens, and (3) the comforting of each other with open and honest hearts. These spiritual precepts continue to be the basis for the work that Bob and I share through our ministry in which we teach people how to put these principles into action within their daily lives.

I am proud of the work that Bob has done in writing this book. He has written it to clarify his learning and to share with the world his experience in this unique and powerful form of ministry. He provides, in an engaging way, the biblical and conceptual underpinnings for this work, while graphically portraying the types of struggles that Christians have in their walks. He effectively articulates the barriers to growing in authenticity with one's self and others and how to overcome these.

I trust that the enclosed insights will be inspiring to your own personal walk with Jesus Christ.

Gary Gemmill, PhD
Professor Emeritus of Organizational Behavior,
Whitman School of Management, Syracuse University
Faculty Coordinator for Leadership and Organization Change,
Walden University
Past Member of the Board of Editors for Small Group Research

Preface

What is it that allows us to understand and connect more sincerely with the people who God blesses our lives with? How about with God himself? What limits our capacity and willingness to do so?

These are the types of questions that I started researching more than a decade ago when, as a graduate student at Syracuse University, I came across a unique management program focused on how people (and groups of people) work together. My fascination with this topic was born not only out of academic interest, but also from the puzzling inconsistencies in my life:

- My secretive, sinful habits that few knew about, certainly not my long-time girlfriend

- My inner discomfort around other people, despite a job that brought me into contact with a wide variety of folks

- My outbursts of anger and selfishness, despite having an abundance of material success

- My pangs of discontent and disinterest with God, despite having been brought up in a loving church environment.

These inconsistencies reached a boiling point as I decided to propose to my girlfriend. I was convinced that I could not be the husband that she deserved if I didn't deal with them, yet I had no idea how to, because I really didn't know how to describe—let alone process—whatever my real issues were.

In circumstances that I now recognize as the guiding hand of our patient, graceful God, a supportive professor noted my interest and invited me to be part of an intense, small-group study that examined practically the balance among each participant's emotional, physical, intellectual, and spiritual gifts.

Through this workshop, I was able to see clearly—for the first time—the roots of my inconsistency. I had never seen "it" before inside of me, but when I recognized "it," it was so obvious that I was able to begin letting "it" go constructively.

As importantly, I was able to understand in far more depth what form this "it" uniquely took within the others in the group, which helped me to better understand and support them in moving forward in their lives—in essence, developing my ability to connect more authentically with others and their experiences.

Now, after many years of further research and analysis on this topic involving hundreds of people, God has been putting an increasing burden on my heart to share these insights. Specifically, my growing realization of how precious it is to give to one another from our gifts leads me to share the following pages with you.

This book documents the powerful observations and results from this research on developing greater empathy and compassion—and in turn, unlocking (or restoring) greater levels of passion, creativity, and wholeness—within ourselves and with those who share our life journey.

In particular, I trust that you will find the enclosed biblically based insights on defining the gradients of compassion, the forms of self-medication that hinder our position and progress within these gradients, and how others have broken through their own barriers to be profoundly helpful for your Christian walk.

I invite you to consider prayerfully taking advantage of the opportunity enclosed within these pages to follow Peter's lead in Matthew 14:27–29 and step out of the boat.

In Christ's love,
Bob Kalka
Georgetown, Texas, USA

Introduction

Do not expect God to cover that which you are not willing to uncover.

—Duncan Campbell[1]

I have not failed. I've just found 10,000 ways that won't work.

—Thomas Edison[2]

Martha[3] called in a state of panic. "I just don't understand," she exclaimed. "No one seems to truly appreciate me—neither my teenage children, my husband, nor anyone in the church. I feel like they all just take advantage of me!"

When Martha had given up a rewarding but hectic professional career in her thirties to become a fortysomething housewife and stay-at-home mother, she looked forward to a fruitful time of meaningful service to her family and church. But instead of finally enjoying a time of family togetherness and marital closeness, Martha perceived an underlying lack of respect from her children, along with her husband's maddening disinterest in this problem. Whenever confronted with her growing frustration, her husband would issue a mumbled protest that he was trying his best and she needed to get off of his case.

But at least she had her church. There always seemed to be an important job that needed to be done, and the congregation was more than happy when she would step up to the task at hand. Martha started to dedicate herself to a wide range of activities that she had previously never had the time for, and she gladly accepted when she was asked to take responsibility for even more prominent projects.

However, as the projects grew in number and importance, Martha began to observe that her fellow volunteers didn't seem quite as committed to the work as she was. She was frequently left in the position of having to step in and handle some delegated tasks herself at the last minute, which meant longer hours at the church. Over time, she sensed that others were taking for granted that she'd always step in to complete the job.

"I don't understand how these people can call themselves Christians," she said. "I'm just trying to be a faithful servant of Christ, and they keep taking advantage of my willingness to help. And then when I get home, my kids give me a hard time, and my husband just sits there. I'm so frustrated and angry. What can I do?"

◆   ◆   ◆

"My wife just doesn't get it," Simon exclaimed. "She says she's Christian, but if she really is, why does she keep giving me a hard time about volunteering at the shelter? We're living an incredibly blessed life these days, and she just doesn't seem to want to lift a finger to help those folks who are *really* in need. If it comes down to my wife or my calling, I don't know what I'll choose."

Since becoming born-again at a Christian men's gathering several years earlier, Simon was making up for lost time. As a salesman, he spent long hours on the road away from his family, but he proudly stepped up to the challenge of being a visible witness for Christ in the secular business world, where the allure of material success often fostered self-indulgent attitudes and behaviors.

Although the experience of witnessing in this environment was at times uncomfortable and unfruitful, Simon was pleased to see how many businesspeople were receptive to the message of Christ. And because he had become familiar with so many different ministries, he enjoyed helping those he met get directly involved in God's work, especially in his home city. Although this meant even more time away from home, he felt that the sanctity of this work justified the additional sacrifice.

But then there was his family. While his children didn't seem to mind his spending some of his nontraveling days doing God's work, his wife clearly didn't understand how important it was to him. Simon said, "I feel so pressured—I don't feel like I can win. If I serve God, my wife gets mad and says that she feels like she's fighting against God for my time, but if I don't serve him, then I feel incredibly guilty. What can I do?"

◆   ◆   ◆

"I feel stuck," lamented Harriet, a technology professional. "God has brought a few wonderful friends into my life, but they frankly pull all of the life right out of me. I never have time for the other things that I want to do because these friends are very needy, and they always seem to call at a bad time. And my husband and I are having some problems, too."

Since leaving the church several years ago, after feeling judged because of her irregular attendance at weekly services, Harriet had been on a personal mission to carry out God's instruction to "love one another" as humbly as she could. Because she had a natural gift for listening, she found it easy to help others who were struggling, to allow them time to vent, as well as consider alternative ways to handle their challenges.

However, Harriet had reached her breaking point. The burdens of taking care of her husband, children, friends, and job were becoming overwhelming, but she felt powerless to pull back from any of her activities and relationships. They were all so important to her.

"I know that some of these relationships aren't healthy, but I have no idea what to do about them. While I don't know why I feel so powerless to make some changes that I know must be made, I am 100 percent sure that my frustration and angst are going to explode sometime soon. What can I do?"

◆   ◆   ◆

All three of these cases, and the countless others like them, reflect the types of challenges that Christians struggle with every day. Our human condition can be seen as a dilemma, with the inherent tension between God-given direction and an innately self-oriented nature that diverts us from doing the compassionate work God truly intends. Repeated observation shows that this conflict can influence patterns and behaviors that have a substantially negative impact on the enthusiasm (passion), imagination (creativity), and unity (wholeness) within our Christian walk.

We often feel that the culpability for our challenges lies primarily with the personally demanding people who God has placed in our lives. However, research confirms that the responsibility also lies within us, in particular from deep-seated inner beliefs that drive us into unproductive yet familiar patterns in our relationships, along with the walls that we construct to keep these beliefs hidden from others and ourselves.

The concealed nature of these walls and beliefs—which are essentially *barriers* that inhibit our ability to sincerely carry out God's will for our lives—explains why simply applying well-intentioned advice from family, friends, and clergy does not generally lead to lasting improvements in these situations.

My purpose here is to share the explicit findings from a long-term research study that clarifies why and how these barriers are constructed, how they can be compassionately deconstructed, and what the resulting benefits are for our Christian walk. In particular, we'll explore how to build an increasingly meaningful and authentic Christian walk by identifying and removing the hidden barriers to experiencing greater passion, creativity, and wholeness within that walk.

The sources of these barriers can be identified through a candid examination of the differences between God's intended plan for us and the reality of how we're living out that plan. In other words, do our actions mirror that which Christ teaches? Consistently, with *everyone* who God has blessed our lives with, especially our spouses and families?

Let's explore this.

Introduction Endnotes

[1] *Men of Integrity* 8, no. 2 (12 March 2005).

[2] Thomas Edison Quotes, http://www.brainyquote.com/quotes/authors/t/thomas_a_edison.html (accessed 16 October 2006).

[3] All names have been changed.

1

The Call to Compassion

Praise be to the God and Father of our Lord Jesus Christ,
the Father of compassion and the God of all comfort,
who comforts us in all our troubles,
so that we can comfort those in any trouble
with the comfort we ourselves have received from God.

—2 Corinthians 1:3–4

I pray also that the eyes of your heart may be enlightened in order that you
may know the hope to which he has called you.

—Ephesians 1:18

Let's begin our inquiry by delving into what can arguably be called the most powerful word in scripture concerning emotional authenticity. That word is compassion.

Compassion is defined by *Webster's Dictionary* as the "sympathetic consciousness of others' distress together with a desire to alleviate it."[4] In other words, compassion involves putting into action the same kind of love that God has for us.

Gradients of Compassion

In our research, we have repeatedly observed four ranges, or gradients, of compassionate outreach, based on each individual's level of awareness of both him/herself and others. These four gradients can be visualized as follows:

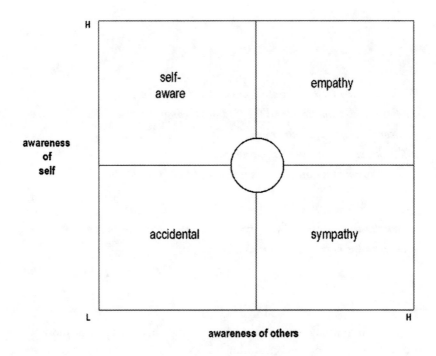

Figure 1: Gradients of Compassion

Let's briefly introduce each gradient.

Accidental

When we have a relatively undeveloped or superficial awareness of both our own and others' experiences, feelings, and emotions, we cannot effectively relate to others' issues and pains.

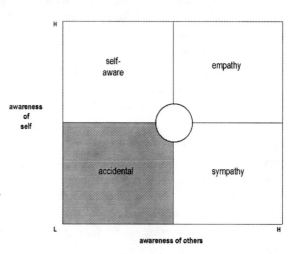

Even in this gradient, however, simple acts of sharing such as common courtesies result in a basic level of compassion.

For example, when I instinctively slow down to let an apparently frantic driver merge onto a crowded freeway, I'm showing a simple form of compassion. Even though I may never realize what was causing the person to drive so frenetically, this basic act of compassion can have a comforting influence on both of us, even if only for a few moments.

Self-Aware

Some of us naturally seek self-awareness. As we become more aware of our own experiences, feelings, and emotions, we are better able to sense and relate to the same in others—as the old adage states, "it takes one to know one." This is fundamentally important, as it enables us to share a form of compassion that is more intimate than accidental.

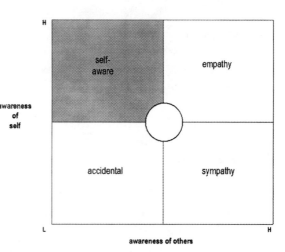

However, a characteristic of this gradient is an imbalance in how we apply our emotional awareness. While our greater self-awareness gives us the *potential* to relate to others more deeply, in this gradient we don't convert that potential into consistent action. Rather, we become self-consumed, fixating on analyzing internally and reacting externally from our self-awareness, while remaining only superficially aware of what others are actually experiencing.

For example, during my earliest research at Syracuse, I became aware of an overpowering sense of internal rage that I had not previously discerned. While this realization clearly gave me a greater potential to relate to similar feelings and emotions in others, as well as the experiences that can lead to them, the several months that I spent alternating between expressing my fury and feeling sorry for myself didn't allow my heart any room to tune into what others around me were experiencing.

I can remember vividly how, during this time, any outreach toward others really stemmed from my own need to develop a better understanding of my rage. As a result, while my efforts to offer compassion at that time were described to be noticeably energetic, my appreciation of others' particular struggles was not well developed.

Sympathy

Some of us are more comfortable learning first through other people. As we strive to become more aware of our family members', friends', and acquaintances' experiences, feelings, and emotions, we enable ourselves to connect more authentically to our own personal awareness.

However, as with self-awareness, this gradient is characterized by an imbalance in how we utilize our

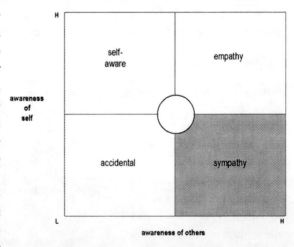

emotional awareness. Here, as we fixate on others, we find ourselves unable or unwilling to connect this growing awareness with our own inner reality, and we remain only superficially aware of our own feelings and emotions.

Trying to solve other people's problems while refusing to acknowledge our own is typical of this gradient, especially as the imbalance grows. Martha, who we met in the last chapter, is a great example of this. She stops at a moment's notice to listen and offer counsel for any problems that someone is willing to share, but she has built walls that prevent her from connecting their experiences with her own in a meaningful way.

As with the previous gradient, our compassion here may be energetic, but others can sense that we struggle to relate to what they're actually experiencing. Although this outreach is important and will likely be appreciated, any impact is typically short-term.

Empathy

As we develop a greater and more balanced awareness of both others and ourselves, we can experience *empathy*. Empathy, which is the ability to relate genuinely with another's pain, is a crucial ingredient for producing compassionate outreach that can have a lasting, and even life-changing, impact.

God feels empathy toward us because he understands us,[5] as he illustrates

through the father's reaction in the parable of the prodigal son.[6] Scripture alludes to empathy as an important characteristic for effective priests, stating "because he is human, he is able to deal gently with the people ... for he is subject to the same weaknesses they have."[7] Likewise, we're all to share this same powerful form of compassion with others.[8]

When our compassion flows out of empathy, we are able to relate more authentically to others because we can connect our own personal awareness effectively with their struggles. Let's look at this gradient further in the following section.

Developing Empathy, Growing Compassion

Our aptitude for empathy influences how dramatic and lasting the impact of our compassionate outreach can be.

Empathy is especially powerful in those times when God blesses our lives with someone who is struggling with feelings of hopelessness in some area of their life. A typical characteristic of hopelessness is an underlying belief that "no one could possibly understand what I'm going through."

Compassion from the accidental, self-awareness or sympathy gradients can't generally change this belief—and in many cases just solidifies it, as others' outreach is taken to be a confirmation that one truly is in a troubled situation.

However, compassion based on empathy allows us to relate in a more powerful and meaningful way. When we share our relevant and connected experiences, feelings, and emotions with the "hopeless," they realize that they really are not "the only one" who has ever experienced their type of situation. This understanding can spark a dramatic transformation of renewed hope, and even a renewed life, through the power of the Holy Spirit.

For example, I spent some time recently with Toby, a middle-aged man who was convinced that his secret, decades-old problem with alcohol and sexual exploits when he traveled for work would inevitably destroy his marriage, family, and even potentially church. Toby was convinced that his situation was hopeless, and that his blatant hypocrisy would soon be found out.

Even though I had frankly never experienced the depth of the perversions that Toby was mired in, the significant work that I had previously done on my own alcohol- and sex-related issues enabled me to help him see that he was not alone in struggling with these topics. Soon after, Toby had a major breakthrough based on the process laid out in this book, and as of this writing he is now over eighteen months into a confident recovery.

It is crucial that we develop our capacity for empathy. What keeps us stuck outside of the empathy gradient? How can we follow a genuine path toward greater empathy?

Our research shows that progressing in our awareness from pure intellectual knowledge to a deeper *understanding* of ours and others' experiences, feelings, and emotions is an essential key to developing empathy.

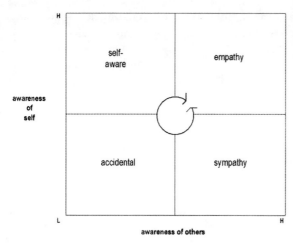

Why is this so important? Let's look at the two possible paths that can lead us toward empathy for any given situation.

Although self-knowledge can help us progress out of the accidental gradient, our initial response is often limited to surface-level behaviors and feelings as we move into self-awareness. However, when our knowledge begins to connect with a deeper understanding of our own experiences, feelings, and emotions, our potential to recognize and relate to others grows considerably, which then positions us to progress into a state of empathy.

To illustrate this path from my own experience, once I allowed myself to discover and work through the primary reasons underlying my rage, this emotion was transformed from an unwelcome crutch into a powerful and ongoing source of deeper understanding of both others and myself. Specifically, as I came to realize its source (i.e. a strong sense of loss from my earlier years), I was able to clearly see how fundamentally this irritation was driving the rebellious activities that I previously shared back in the preface … and how others could be affected in a similar way.

Likewise, although knowledge of others' experiences, feelings, and emotions can help us progress from the accidental gradient into the sympathy gradient, our ability to relate these with our own understanding is not automatic, especially if we tend to emotionally isolate ourselves. However, as we gain a deeper understanding of others' reality, and then begin to relate this with similarities in our own experiences, we are then capable of moving into empathy.

The primary goal of this book is to detail an experiential process for developing greater empathy out of our own unique experiences, feelings, and emotions. This is, in essence, a process of developing emotional wisdom.

Godly wisdom actually is defined by three elements—not only knowledge and understanding, but also *obedience*.[9] Thus, to grow in our capacity to share ourselves more authentically, we cannot only focus on building knowledge and understanding. We must also put our awareness into consistent, loving action.

Let's look at how to accomplish this.

Chapter Endnotes

[4] *Webster's Ninth New Collegiate Dictionary* (Springfield, MA: Merriam-Webster, 1988), p. 268.

[5] Psalms 103:13–14; Hebrews 4:14–16.

[6] Luke 15:11–24.

[7] Hebrews 5:2 (NLT).

[8] 2 Corinthians 1:4–5.

[9] Proverbs 4:5, 7.

2

God's Intention

The most important commandment is this ...
'The Lord our God is the one and only Lord.
And you must love the Lord your God with all your heart,
all your soul, all your mind, and all your strength.'

The second is equally important:
'Love your neighbor as yourself.'
No other commandment is greater than these.

—Mark 12:29–31

The Holy Bible is an incredible book in so many ways, with its wisdom, instruction, history, songs, prophecy, and other remarkable content. It is also incredible in terms of length! Newer Christians, as well as other curious readers, will at times pick up some translation of the word of God and wonder where to start, given its composition as one of the largest books that they've probably ever read from.

With more than 750,000 words in the Bible, living by the word of God can seem overwhelming, especially as its endless breadth of wisdom shines upon our limited human perspective. Yet scripture states, "Man [shall live] by *every word* that comes from the mouth of God."[10] We sometimes start to wonder what ties all of these words together?

Fortunately, scripture provides a "Cliffs Notes" version of itself within itself, because it boils all of God's revelations down to their core intention. As stated so clearly in the twelfth chapter of Mark, as well as the twenty-second chapter of Matthew, we're all to:

10

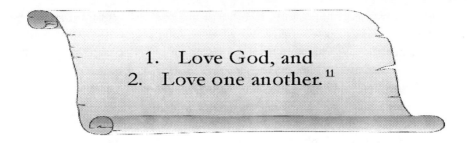

> 1. Love God, and
> 2. Love one another.[11]

That's all there is to it, short and sweet—our God-given "divine plan," a life-giving design that provides healthy, fruitful meaning for our lives. As Jesus Christ states so boldly about these two points, "All the Law and the Prophets hang on these two commandments."[12] That is, every law, story, prophecy, parable, and statement in both the Old and New Testaments serve to help us understand just *how* we're to love him and one another.

And we must need *lots* of help, given the amount of scripture he's given to us!

Scripture identifies several characteristics that should guide our lives as we carry out God's divine plan. Seeking these qualities and putting them into practice enables us to live in a way that is more consistent with his intentions:

Compassion.[13] Love is not only a feeling—it is a decision and action to meet another's needs. Do we reach out and love one another, even our enemies, without the self-absorbed, "What's in it for me?" love that pervades the world today?[14] While every act of love admittedly feeds both ourselves and others, we're to "do nothing out of selfish ambition or vain conceit, but in humility consider others better than" ourselves.[15] As Jesus did, we're "not (to) preach ourselves, but Jesus Christ as Lord, and ourselves as your servants,"[16] while we "open wide" our hearts to each other.[17] As stated in the last chapter, the more powerful forms of compassion require some level of awareness both of ourselves and others—as our awareness of both develop, we're better able to understand and thus help with others' situations and struggles, not to mention more constructively deal with our own.

Responsiveness. Do we love God and one another out of gratitude for Jesus's incredible sacrifice on Calvary for every one of us, or do we do this out of a misguided quest to earn enough points to get through the gates of heaven someday? Jesus states, "You did not choose me, but I chose you."[18]

Generosity. Do we faithfully build upon God's blessings for us into obedient service with and toward others, or do we complacently hoard these blessings to ourselves? As Paul states to the church in Corinth, "Whoever sows sparingly will also reap sparingly, and whoever sows generously will also reap generously."[19] To the church in Rome, he says, "[in] contributing to the needs of others, let him give generously,"[20] with the original Greek word equating generosity with simplicity—that is, a sincere[21] act unencumbered by hidden motives. Paul also notes to the Galatians, "The one who sows to please his sinful nature, from that nature will reap destruction; the one who sows to please the (Holy) Spirit, from the Spirit will reap eternal life."[22] The more of ourselves we invest in loving God and others with true compassion in response to his priceless gift of Jesus as the payment for our sins, the more he is able to bless us in return.[23]

These three factors are critical. However, they are incomplete because they do not tell us how to personalize the way in which we carry out God's divine plan. Scripture instructs us to do this by using the unique set of God-given gifts he has blessed us with.[24] As the New Testament letter known as First Peter states, "Each one should use whatever gift he has received to serve others, faithfully administering God's grace."[25] Said differently,

> We are to obediently[26] share his gifts *compassionately* and *generously*,[27] which he provides out of his unmerited love and favor for us (i.e., grace), in order to love one another in *response* to his great gift of eternal life.

In particular, God gives us the *intellectual, physical, spiritual,* and *emotional* gifts that we need to do the work he intends us to do. And all four are crucial. As one source observes, "The Christian life ... requires the commitment of one's whole being to Jesus—body, mind, emotions, and will ..."[28]

> **Intellectually**, he blesses us with the capability to seek him out critically. Through the gifts of knowledge and teaching,[29] we can be transformed by learning more fully about his goodness,[30] how to live out his teachings in our lives, and how to share them effectively within an increasingly secular and idolatrous world.

> **Physically**, he blesses us with the miracle of the human body. Not only are we given skills such as speaking and serving,[31] but he also establishes incredible self-correcting mechanisms within our bodies. For example, regardless of our nutrition and lifestyle choices, our bodies will normally do everything possible to stay in a good working order.

Spiritually, he provides us with a counselor[32] in the Holy Spirit, who guides us closer to himself through the change-inducing fruit of love, joy, peace, and so on.[33] He also blesses us with a variety of gifts to assist others to come closer to him—capabilities such as discerning godly wisdom, prophesying, miraculous powers and healing, the distinguishing between spirits, the gift of tongues, and—of course—faith.[34] This awesome Spirit is arguably the most tangible evidence we have of God's presence in our lives today. For example, as we experience the deep, soulful peace that comes from a growing personal relationship with God, that peace stands in remarkable contrast with our former understanding of peace, which was likely defined as positive thinking or a temporary lack of conflict. Or, as we humbly answer God's call to share our unique gifts—for example, a gift of leadership or administration—our anointing can lead others (as well as ourselves) to become increasingly aware of the Holy Spirit's presence.

Emotionally, God gives us each a heart that is capable of a regenerating wellspring of compassionate, responsive, and generous love. Christianity is a religion of the heart. As scripture states, God "will give you a new heart; [he] will remove from you your heart of stone and give you a heart of flesh,"[35] so that once "you have purified yourselves by obeying the truth so that you have sincere love for your brothers, [you can] love one another deeply, from the heart."[36] We're instructed to nurture and protect our hearts,[37] because scripture tells us that this is where God's peace actually lives within us.[38]

One of the most important functions God has blessed our hearts with is the intriguing ability to *connect* directly with others' hearts, to share the love from within us effectively. This phenomenon in action, which can be termed *emotional intimacy,* enables us to share God's gifts, such as encouragement, mercy and compassion, and even leadership,[39] in a way that positively affects others.

Connecting with God's People

Unlike the worldly definition of intimacy, which usually is defined as a highly personal and often sexual relationship, emotional intimacy covers a broad spectrum of connections between people. Specifically, one can assert five levels of connectedness,[40] from superficial to intensely deep. The levels include:

1. *Acknowledgment.* Have you ever seen someone you recognize but don't really know that well? And as your eyes lock for a moment, you both

quietly share a smile or nod of the head? This is the most ritualized form of emotional intimacy. It may seem simple and innocuous, but we all realize how powerful this form can be after someone we know turns away after seeing us without offering such a greeting.

2. *Small Talk.* Sometimes referred to as the "evening news" level of emotional connection, this is where we converse with others about the types of things that could appear on television news programs. This type of connection is important, as it brings spoken conversation into a relationship for the first time, even if it often takes a somewhat trivial form. It is also the level that some people often have a hard time moving past because of the vulnerability and openness that characterize the levels beyond this one.

3. *Sharing Opinions.* Here, we begin sharing our beliefs. This type of connection introduces personal risk for the first time, as we begin to reveal our attitudes and outlook, which we worry others will think are strange, excessive, or simply wrong. This is the level where evangelistic outreach efforts often start to conflict with the world, because sharing God's absolute offer of salvation is an increasingly risky assertion within a secular society that evaluates everything from a relative point of view. [41]

4. *Sharing Feelings.* Here, we begin sharing our inner passions, joys, and pains, which introduces even more personal risk than the previous levels. We worry, often based on past experiences, that others may use this personal information to manipulate or embarrass us, or worse yet, invalidate our feelings in some way.

5. *Unhindered Intimacy.* In this, the deepest level, we let down even the most top-secret inner walls that we have built to cope with the life experiences that we've been unable to process fully. This is typically a level that is visited infrequently and only for very short periods because it is so intensely personal and exposing—yet crucial for growing beyond our hidden barriers. For example, one might confront some decades-old pain with a parent in an honest attempt to move beyond some self-defeating pattern of living, despite risking a tenuous status quo within the family. Or, a spouse may disclose an inappropriate relationship in a confession and cry for repentance to relieve his or her deep guilt in an attempt to build long-term sustainability into the marriage, despite a very real risk of painful short-term consequences.

The following illustration represents this paradigm of emotional intimacy:

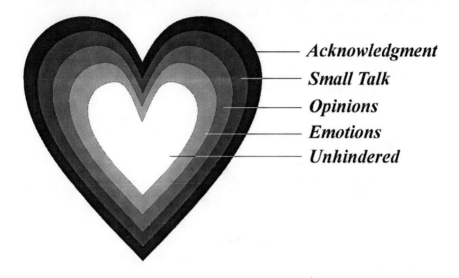

Acknowledgment

Small Talk

Opinions

Emotions

Unhindered

Figure 2: The Five Levels of Emotional Intimacy

With this paradigm in mind, it is important to consider how we can love one another most effectively. Our initial goal should be to connect with others at the level of emotional intimacy that *they need,* not at the level that *we want,* because we could be shifting responsibility for our own issues to others in the latter case. Self-centeredness is not appropriate here, as with the other areas of our Christian walk.

For example, let's say that I'm building a relationship with someone who I can sense is struggling with a specific emotional pain. Although my head may try to steer me away from discussing similar feelings that I've experienced and dealt with in the past, because I worry that the conversation will take more than the few minutes that my busy calendar allows, my heart may tell me that doing so would be the most compassionate way to meet this other person's need. If I follow this latter path, then the wisdom and love that God has poured within me has a chance to be a balm for this hurting soul. If I instead reject this opportunity, and on the way out the door hurriedly share my opinion that this person is a wonderful person and that I'm sure he or she will be able to handle it with God's help, then I will have shared little to no compassion.

Alternatively, what if my path crosses repeatedly with someone who has become deeply emotionally scarred through years of abuse from a series of perpetually manipulative partners? This person may feel increasingly alone, because he or she believes that anyone who tries to get close will become emotionally abusive, which leads to a refusal to let anyone into a deeper level of intimacy. Although I may want to prove that not everyone will become emo-

tionally abusive when given the chance, it may be more loving to engage in simple small talk with this person until he or she indicates a readiness to go deeper—regardless of how long that takes. We must be sure that any call that we feel to help this person doesn't actually reinforce his or her issue and any defense mechanisms that stem from it.

When we are truly connected to another human being at the appropriate level—that is, based on the other's need—then we are able to fulfill God's divine plan more effectively through sharing our gifts with compassion, responsiveness, and generosity. When we reach this effective state of connection with someone, then God's love has a greater potential to be visibly reflected through our hearts.

So why do others so often find it difficult to see God's light clearly reflected through our hearts?

Certainly one reason is others' inability or unwillingness to work on their own issues, which can impede them from understanding or accepting God's love expressed through us. Here, our role is to simply continue loving them however possible. Similar to the experience of the prodigal son's father, we cannot force others to address their own issues, nor should we ever make the mistake of trying to solve others' emotional issues.[42] Only they can permit and accomplish this.

We can, however, work on another common reason, which is our own weakness in reflecting God's love transparently.[43] Regardless of how much progress others make on their own emotional issues, if we are not reflecting God's love clearly, then others will obviously have a hard time seeing its life-changing power. At its extreme, a dim reflection of Christ's love may even be used as the excuse that others cling to in order to justify continued denial and avoidance of their own issues.

Although both of these reasons are typically active in any difficult relationship, sensibly understanding and addressing the latter issue—our shortcomings—will be our focus in the following chapters. Observation shows that such exploration can lead to substantial improvement in our ability to love others more authentically, while fundamentally improving the passion, creativity, and wholeness within our own personal relationship with Jesus Christ. Many of the same things that influence the quality of our relationships with others also affect our relationship with the Lord.

Chapter Endnotes

[10] Matthew 4:4.

[11] Mark 12:29–31; Matthew 22:37–40; 1 John 4:7–21.

[12] Matthew 22:40.

[13] Colossians 3:12.

[14] Mark 2:3; Romans 12:14.

[15] Philippians 2:3.

[16] 2 Corinthians 4:5.

[17] 2 Corinthians 6:13.

[18] John 15:16.

[19] 2 Corinthians 9:6.

[20] Romans 12:8.

[21] Romans 12:9.

[22] Galatians 6:8.

[23] Matthew 13:12, 25:29.

[24] Romans 12:6.

[25] 1 Peter 4:10.

[26] 1 John 2:5.

[27] 1 Peter 4:10 (NLT); 2 Corinthians 9:10–13.

[28] *Our Daily Bread* 50, no. 3 (27 June 2005).

[29] Romans 12:7.

[30] Romans 12:2.

[31] 1 Peter 4:11.

[32] John 14:16–17.

[33] Galatians 5:22–23.

[34] 1 Peter 4:10–12; Romans 12:4–8; 1 Corinthians 12:4–10; Matthew 9:35–38.

[35] Ezekiel 36:26.

[36] 1 Peter 1:22.

[37] Proverbs 4:23.

[38] Colossians 3:15.

[39] 1 Peter 4:10–12; Romans 12:4–8; 1 Corinthians 12:4–10; Matthew 9:35–38.

[40] Derived from *The Five Levels of Intimacy* from The Smalley Relationship Center, http://www.familyfirst.net/marriage/intimacylevels.asp (accessed 9 March 2007).

[41] "Americans Are Most Likely to Base Truth on Feelings," The Barna Group, http://www.barna.org/FlexPage.aspx?Page=BarnaUpdate&BarnaUpdateID=106 (accessed 13 March 2007).

[42] Luke 15:11–20.

[43] 2 Corinthians 3:18.

3

My Reality

Now we see but a poor reflection as in a mirror ...

—*1 Corinthians 13:12a*

Your life either sheds light or casts a shadow.

—*Author Unknown*

What I am is God's gift to me; what I do with it is my gift to Him

—*Warren Wiersbe*[44]

Can others see a transparent, clear reflection of God's love through my life?

Or do they see a faint, grainy reflection?

Or do they strain to see any light at all that can be attributed to God? Do they conclude, based on comparing my observable actions with my claims to be a Christian, that my God must represent selfishness, hypocrisy, criticism, pretense, or sinful compromise?

> For example, while Martha (who was discussed in the Introduction) saw herself as a committed, faithful servant of Christ, her husband and children saw an overstressed, emotionally disengaged wife and mother who would consistently isolate herself for hours each day to work off her tension—after she pulled herself away from church long enough to return home.

Because of our sinful nature, which encourages us to please ourselves rather than God, we constantly struggle against veiling God's reconciling light—Jesus Christ.[45] John states, "If we claim to be without sin, we deceive ourselves and the truth is not in us."[46] As Paul illustrates so painfully well, "I do not understand what I do. For what I want to do I do not do, but what I hate I do. For I have the desire to do what is good, but I cannot carry it out."[47]

Let's look further at the relationship between sin—our own as well as others'—and its impact on our Christian walk.

Sin and Suffering

Sin can lead to physical suffering, often through ailments caused directly by the sinful act, as well as through related stress. Here, God blesses us with the wonders of medicine, therapy, and natural healing to assist with our pain.

Sin can also lead to intellectual suffering, as knowledge of God and his wisdom reveals the errors in our ways, and we deal with the consequences of these blunders on others and ourselves.

Sin can also lead to spiritual suffering, by placing distance between God's heavenly fruit and us.[48] Accepting Jesus within our hearts opens up the bridge that spans this gap for us, while being obedient to his teachings enables us to cross that bridge. As we are reconciled with this spiritual fruit, we are in turn better able to assist others with their own similar suffering.

And sin can obviously lead to emotional suffering. First, we experience the short-term highs that often accompany the act of sinning. But after the high has worn off, we are often left with longer-lasting feelings such as disappointment, frustration, loneliness, anger, inadequacy, guilt, shame, or sadness. These residual feelings affect both us and others who are directly or indirectly affected by this sin.

Because these enduring feelings are troubling—and thus uncomfortable—we are inclined to distance ourselves from them, or even try to ignore them completely. When we refuse to take ownership of such feelings, we essentially invent a fantasy about ourselves. If we continue to disown these feelings, even if we've confessed any related sin, we feed a form of emotional inertia that encourages us to maintain this fabricated reality. Over time, it becomes increasingly difficult to acknowledge that the disowned emotions even exist within us.

> For example, Matt is a longtime church member and family man who has struggled for years with a recurring bubble of anger that always seems to rear its ugly head in public at the most inopportune times. This leads to critical whispers and gossip in the community, which triggers ongoing feelings of shame and sadness. Although Matt had been in a constant state of introspection about his angry temperament, spending an admirable amount of time praying about his anger, any results were always short lived, which led to fur-

ther frustration for him—and additional rounds of anger. What Matt had been trying to avoid was a growing realization that his anger was actually covering up a deeper emotion—in his case, a profound sadness rooted in emotionally significant incidents during his teenage years that he had not been willing to process.

The psalmist writes, "But you desire honesty from the heart, so you can teach me to be wise in my inmost being."[49] What a disappointing form of pride that we, who are saved by Jesus's sacrifice and obedience, would march down our own path and pretend that ignoring our own emotional reality is helpful. In fact, this approach conflicts with the scriptural command that our love is to be without *dissimulation*,[50] which means we should not conceal the truth about our feelings under a false appearance.[51]

Behavioral Effects

The problems with emotional avoidance are obvious. How can we authentically relate to others' issues if we're unwilling to acknowledge and learn from our own similar issues?

But, we exclaim, "God certainly doesn't want *me* to feel *bad*," and we continue trying to ignore these feelings. This begs one of the most consequentially significant sets of questions that we may ever ask ourselves:

1. Would an all-loving God actually allow us to experience things that make us feel *bad*? Over a long period of time? *On purpose?*

2. Could these emotions—and *dealing* with them—be part of the sufferings that Jesus says we'll have to experience in order to follow him?

3. And even crazier, could they actually be *gifts* from God himself?

We typically respond with an emphatic "no," despite scripture that encourages us toward a different conclusion.[52] So we continue trying to ignore what is stirring within us, despite still feeling those deep-down pangs of incompleteness that form emotional holes at the bottom of our souls that we so maddeningly are unable or unwilling to see into.

Worse yet, as situations occur that tap into these disowned feelings, we must spend even more time and effort maintaining our fabricated reality. "Pain avoidance" becomes our standard reaction to the *other* challenging emotions that arise in our lives.

And the breadth of our fantasy grows even further.

In other words, we institutionalize our refusal to acknowledge our deepest uncomfortable emotions, despite their presence within us. This break between our true feelings and the idealized image we construct about ourselves forms these holes that we have to work increasingly hard to manage, as we try to avoid people and places we fear could shine an unwelcome light toward the disowned parts within us.

And, as we then increasingly "pre-qualify" that which we might be exposed to—and stay away from that which we subconsciously worry could touch upon our disowned imperfections and unresolved emotions—we naturally begin trying to exert more control over who and what we'll allow ourselves to experience. Eventually, even the selected people and places that we let into our comfort zone begin to tap into our buried emotions, regardless of our best efforts. So we simply continue to narrow this zone down into a severely constrained set of people, places, and feelings.

Not surprisingly, this narrowing process often leads us to develop an intense desire for predictability among those people and places still inside our comfort zone. Sometimes this desire encourages strong controlling behaviors, such as holding others responsible for our happiness, and then justifying sinful behaviors when they fail. This cycle is a guaranteed outcome because we ourselves are the only ones who can make the changes needed to find a place that God's peace and joy can live within.

- For example, people-pleasers will sometimes go overboard in doing things for others in order to seek a constant "fix" of personal affirmation. When people realize that the people-pleaser's service and attention is really fueled by a self-centered agenda and that his or her "fix" can never be fully satisfied, they will often begin to resent the service, which the people-pleaser then views as a fundamental lack of appreciation that justifies any subsequent sinful responses.

- For others, this desire for predictability is transformed into a stubborn unwillingness to let anyone past the first few levels of emotional intimacy. One illustration of this dynamic occurs when the hidden issues are not completely ignored, but acknowledged only at a superficial level where they become an intellectual discussion to be philosophized over endlessly. This can lead to a "predictable unpredictability" within relationships, where others give up trying to build a deeper relationship with us out of puzzled frustration.

- Still others become terminally cynical and judgmental, enthusiastically criticizing others at seemingly every turn. Ironically, this critique is often focused on the same issues that they've hidden inside themselves in an attempt to subconsciously deflect these issues' presence within.

All of these avoidance-oriented reactions are unproductive for our Christian walk. Think about it this way—if Jesus had used *his* power to avoid the emotional (and other) sufferings he knew he would experience,[53] then after blaming God for making things too tough for him, or superficially rationalizing to an understanding public that he just wasn't up to paying the price for *all* of their sins, we would all still be doomed to destruction by God's law.

Over time, avoidance leads us to become emotionally handicapped, if not eventually dead, within our relationships. We simply "go through the motions," unable to be fully engaged in the moment with others—or ourselves. The scriptural command that we share our gifts with each other "so that in all things God may be praised through Jesus Christ"[54] becomes a perplexing fantasy. Paradoxically, our holes become "full"—of feelings of emptiness.

And we wonder where the passion, creativity, and wholeness have disappeared to in our walk with Jesus Christ—with our marriages, children, families, friends, acquaintances, strangers, jobs, church and ministries, and faith?

Obviously, if unaddressed, the holes—and the accompanying emptiness within us—remain. Regardless of how much we try to project, rationalize, or otherwise ignore them, the holes don't simply evaporate. Not after a week. Not after a year. Not after we become an adult. Not when we reach retirement.

How We Cope

Because we aren't generally willing to admit to living inside of a self-constrained emotional comfort zone, we have to cope somehow. As previously stated, the coping mechanism of choice for the vast majority of us is to avoid—that is, ignore or hide—our painful emotions. Yet because the pangs of emptiness that inevitably creep out are not comfortable, let alone welcomed, *we begin to search for ways to effectively medicate ourselves against these feelings*. We attempt to cover our emotional holes with metaphoric fig leaves[55] that will conveniently (yet only temporarily) mask the emptiness.

This self-medication generally takes form as an unhealthy consumption of things that are ironically God-given gifts intended to build up and honor his kingdom. Although most of these gifts are meant to be enjoyed at reasonable levels, misconsuming them becomes toxic. The amount of time that we think about, prepare for, apply, and deal with the consequences of using (or not using) these gifts becomes disproportionately great. And as this unhealthy consumption becomes a more significant priority within our life, and possibly even becomes the primary fuel that we use in attempts to transform our emptiness into wholeness, we essentially enter into a self-centered, potentially abusive, and ultimately idolatrous state.[56]

Which gifts are typically misconsumed? Ask yourself if any of the following sound familiar:

Alcohol and Drugs	Do I seek to avoid the realities in my life through abusing substances, as warned against in scripture,[57] or do I seek lasting inner peace and joy? These substances include alcohol, prescription drugs, and illegal drugs. As an illustration, a person who used illegal drugs was quoted as saying, "I'd always felt that there was a hole inside me. (Methamphetamine) filled it up. I became Superman with my work, and my self-esteem just shot through the roof."[58] Or, do I refuse to take needed medication despite its benefits to perpetuate some level of physical or emotional pain, as a diversion against or proxy for dealing with my deeper, more painful underlying emotions?
Sex	Do I enslave myself to worldly passion[59] instead of honoring God with my body? This includes adultery, pornography, and even the misuse of marital lovemaking by a spouse, if used for one-sided escapism from dealing with crucial issues. Or, do I excuse myself from enjoying the gift of physical intimacy within marriage in a quest to punish myself or my spouse or both for some actual or perceived past misdeeds, or to create a diversion against or proxy for dealing with my deeper, more painful underlying emotions?
Food	Do I take a self-centered or self-punishing view toward food[60], which can produce a variety of physical, emotional, intellectual, and spiritual problems—whether from overeating or undereating?

**Connecting
with Others:**

Gossip   As I develop and experience various levels of emotional intimacy with others, do I often gossip about others or engage in other "godless chatter" to keep the focus off of myself and my own issues?[61]

Venting   Do I often let my emotions get the better of me? For example, do I give "full vent to (my) anger,"[62] or consistently use my emotions to manipulate or attack others, to keep the focus off of myself and my own issues?

Idolatry   Do I hold others responsible for my self-worth and happiness, instead of resting in God's assurance that I cannot earn his approval, because I'm created in his image just below heavenly beings and my sins have been completely separated from me by Jesus Christ?[63]

Projection   Do I try to deflect my emotional reality onto another person or persons—commonly termed *projection*—which is essentially criticizing and attacking others as an outlet for a similar pain or pressure that I'm feeling inside? This enables me to temporarily avoid taking ownership for what is truly within myself, while justifying feelings of frustration and anger toward the person(s) whom I'm projecting onto. This can even lead to condemning[64] the person(s) I'm projecting onto or lashing out at innocent bystanders with the negative feelings that I blame the projectee(s) for. The condemnation and crucifixion of Jesus Christ is the ultimate example of this dynamic.

A false inner belief of "unfixability" is commonly projected. It is far easier and more attractive to focus on fixing or protecting others—and then writing them off if they don't respond to my help—than focusing on my own concealed belief that I'm broken and cannot be fixed. Of course, I *cannot* fix anyone else. I can only work on addressing my own issues and false beliefs, such as the mistaken belief that I must meet certain standards or be approved by certain others to be lovable, or that I'm unworthy of being loved because of past failure.[65]

Rationalizing	Do I try to delude myself into thinking that intellectually acknowledging my troubling emotions is the same as dealing with their underlying impact on my life? Let's face it—admitting that one drinks too much is clearly not the same as getting treatment for an alcoholic condition! With rationalization, I essentially stop at intellectual agreement that the emotion exists within myself, instead of trusting God to help me constructively proceed through this troubling valley. This response commonly stems from several causes: a lack of trust that God can refresh and renew me through the pain; a simple desire to avoid any type of pain, real or perceived; an underlying false belief that I cannot change; or a fear that I might actually be at least somewhat responsible for causing or perpetuating the issue, so I don't want to face any inner guilt.[66]
Withdrawing	Withdrawing emotionally is an underconsumption of connection with others. Do I, like the Israelites described in Isaiah,[67] refuse to accept and deal with bad news, so I'm unable to even begin to address the issues in my life productively, let alone be comforted by his Spirit? Do I shut down emotionally when things start to get tough? Do I pretend that everything is OK when it is not? Do realize that when I check out, I not only put myself at risk of sinning, but also may have a hard time simply recognizing God's presence, analogous to the two men walking from Jerusalem to Emmaus after Jesus' crucifixion?[68]
Entertainment and Leisure	Have entertainment and leisure become my primary occupation? Do I spend hours every day in front of the television watching soap operas, sitcoms, or sports? Surfing the Internet? Shopping? Golfing? Do I spend far more time on these pursuits than I spend in filling my mind with what is good, such as scripture and loving others compassionately? Am I not bothered by the Barna Group's research study that reports that "born again adults spend an average of seven times more hours each week watching television than they do participating in spiritual pursuits such as Bible reading, prayer and worship, spend roughly twice as much money on entertainment as they donate to their church, and spend more time surfing the Net than they do conversing with God in prayer?"[69] Or, do I refuse to partake in entertainment and leisure activities in order to control my environment or make a self-righteous statement as a diversion against or proxy for dealing with my deeper, more painful underlying emotions?

Work	Am I like the Israelites in Exodus, who gave up their God-ordered rest to gather more manna, despite God's assurances that they would have enough? Do I ignore Solomon's wisdom that "toilsome labor" for its own sake is meaningless, instead of resting comfortably in the presence of Jesus Christ?[70] Or, do I hold back from fully committing myself to meaningful work as a type of protest against some injustice that I feel has been perpetuated on me? Does my attitude become a diversion against or proxy for dealing with my deeper, more painful underlying emotions?
Laws	Do I rely on adhering to a set of religious or secular laws or rituals as the basis for my salvation and worth, despite the scriptural statement that faith alone leads to salvation?[71] Or, am I more comfortable living in perpetual rebellion against established scriptural or civil laws as a diversion against or proxy for dealing with my deeper, more painful underlying emotions, regardless of the eventual consequences?

Do I fill every available moment in my life with a frenzied level of service in a quest to find God's peace and joy, instead of patiently serving others out of the peace and joy he's already blessed me with? Do I do this to avoid looking inside myself at how I sincerely feel?

Or, do I serve as a form of idolatry in order to gain affirmation from certain others as a mandate on my self-worth? This shows up in a wide range of dynamics—from an obsession with being a people-pleaser (where I require affirmation in return for my service, or that person is critiqued or cast out), which clearly puts me at risk of going against Jesus' teachings;[72] to being a "time martyr," where I give up that which God wants me to do and instead allow my time to be overly consumed by codependent folks whose continued presence I rely on for self-worth.

Serving and Ministry

Who am I really serving? Do I serve others primarily for the glory of God, or do I serve primarily for self-centered reasons?

At its extreme, within arguably the most respected pursuit of all, does my family struggle to get enough of my undivided time and attention because of my considerable levels of ministry-related activities? Do they feel like they're "fighting God" to get time with me? Christ gave himself up for the church, just as I'm to give myself up for my spouse, putting nothing in the way of accomplishing this—including ministry that in the innermost recesses is really primarily pursuing either approval and affirmation, or removal of some feeling of guilt. A good example of this is Eli in the Old Testament. His focus on ministry, at the expense of his family, led to grave consequences.[73]

Or, do I refuse to serve others or take part in formal ministry or both as a protest against the hypocrisy that I identify in others, especially those in the church? This becomes a self-righteous platform against or proxy for dealing with my deeper, more painful underlying emotions.

Further Observations

Misconsumption leads to other problems as well. For example, if we overconsume, we often introduce consequential issues, as much of our time is then spent on additional consumption just to *maintain or protect* previous consumption. How much time, money, and effort do we spend on protecting what we have and satisfying ourselves materially, instead of using our gifts to reach out with Christ's love, grace, and mercy?

On the other hand, underconsuming these gifts can lead to a state of inaction, where even healthy consumption of these gifts is accompanied by feelings of guilt, along with the fear that we will be unable to stop increasing our usage if we start. This fear is actually warranted in some cases, when the effects of underconsuming are being used as a decoy from dealing with our hidden issues. If this decoy loses its potency as we allow ourselves to enjoy the underconsumed gift, overconsuming that same gift can become a replacement diversion.

Specific types of misconsumption can introduce additional unproductive influences—and a need to deal with the consequences of these—on our Christian walk. For example:

- Misconsumption of the gifts of alcohol or prescription drugs can leave us physically or mentally ill or introduce people who negatively influence the lives of ourselves and our families.

- Misconsumption of the gift of sex can lead to marital strife by instigating selfish habits and perversions, such as pornography and adulterous relationships.

- Misconsumption of the gift of food can lead to a mental and physical state that is constantly distracted by the allure and effects of eating.

- Misconsumption of the gift of connecting with others can lead to emotional (and other forms of) adultery, and/or introduce controlling people who try to divert us from our walk and cause us to miss out on the joy of fellowship.

Misconsumption of any of our God-given gifts can also lead to self-righteous pride, which Christ warns us against in the parable of the equally paid workers.[74] Pride, and its far-reaching toxic effects, eventually leads us into forms of burnout that have an enormous impact on our Christian walk.

For example, the misconsumption of ministry and serving can lead to burnout or withholding of natural gifts and talents. This can hurt or destroy others' understanding of Christianity. How?

Take the case of well-meaning Christians who start a ministry, such as leading an Alpha course[75] or a singles' outreach, but quickly realize that they are leading it for reasons that no longer feel as compelling as they initially did. Because of other commitments, they find that they have really only made a pseudo-commitment to this work and are not prepared to dedicate sufficient prayer and preparation to the effort. As they then either check out mentally and just go through the motions, or abandon the ministry altogether, those who felt led into this ministry are left hurt, confused, and even lost, while the fallout from the ministry's implosion can affect others' willingness to consider Christ for hope and salvation.

In its worst form, our misconsumption becomes on outright addiction that becomes our life's sole focus at the expense of God's desire that we properly use his gifts to love him and each other. This becomes especially problematic if God leads the person who supports our misconsumption to cut us off, because a natural tendency is simply switch to someone else who will support our habits. For example, if you and your spouse misconsume in a certain area, but your spouse successfully turns away from it and then seeks to help you out of it as well, you might lash out at him or her while reaching out to someone else who still shares this same misconsumption, which can obviously have disastrous consequences.

This is the bottom line of our fallen human condition from the emotional point of view: When we spend much of our time self-medicating and dealing with the consequences of these habits on ourselves and others, instead of dealing with the real root issues that could free us from this emotional bondage, how can we possibly focus more on loving one another with authentic compassion? How can we sacrificially center ourselves on what is good, as scripture commands?[76]

Trading Up

Be warned that the solution may not be as simple as addressing the form of misconsumption that we're currently most aware of. Because self-medication is a form of self-deception that increases our vulnerability to further diversion, we must always be on guard for a commonly observed dynamic of *trading up,* where we exchange our excessive misconsumption in one area for misconsumption in another form that is perceived to be more acceptable socially. For example, while the overconsumption of alcohol is seen as negative by virtually everyone, a workaholic or "churchaholic" is often respected, if not openly praised, in many societies.

> To illustrate "trading up" in action, let's return to Simon (whom we met in the Introduction). In his early twenties, after recognizing unresolved anger toward his parents and its link to his self-medicative habits, he was able to eliminate his consumption of illegal drugs and extramarital sex. However, rather than complete the work needed to achieve greater authenticity, he simply traded up for an overconsumption of work. After being confronted with his workaholism several years later, he confessed but again traded up to a "better" form, in this case involvement in several active Christian ministries. It took Simon several more years to recognize this pattern for what it

was, but when he did, he was finally able to do the necessary work (detailed later in this book) to discover greater authenticity and refocus his efforts to love others—beginning at home with his long-suffering (and not surprisingly, initially hesitant) wife and kids.

A fascinating recent study illustrates this point well. Today, gastric bypass surgery is an incredibly popular, "fast-path" method for weight loss, with about 140,000 such operations taking place each year in the United States. However, reports note that between 5 and 30 percent of people who go through this type of operation end up adopting a new addictive behavior to replace their former over-consumption of food.[77]

Misconsumption forms a mask that hides the true state of our hearts from ourselves and those in our lives. As we wear this mask on a continual basis, we ironically end up protecting ourselves from realizing our true God-intended selves. Instead of our walk with Christ reflecting God's light to a world that desperately needs it, his light becomes diffused as it struggles to not be fully consumed within our emotional holes, sometimes to the degree that little or no light can be seen on the outside.

Impact on Intimacy

Ultimately, the most observable consequence of emotional avoidance is a pattern of problems with intimacy among the people who God has placed in our lives. If we choose to self-medicate rather than face our disowned feelings, we aren't likely to let anyone else see our hidden holes—at least on purpose! This is problematic because actively sharing our lives with others inevitably leads to situations and conversations that tap into what has been disowned, whether by chance or purposefully through intervention.

A good scriptural illustration of this is Jesus with the woman at the well. When Jesus confronted her about her marital status, implicitly pointing out that none of her previous relationships had filled her emptiness, she quickly tried to change the subject back to Christ.[78] When we sense others are beginning to get too close to that which we will not allow ourselves to see, we erect barriers. And if others refuse to stay behind these barriers, we often start actively pushing them out—even if in subtle ways, such as manipulating our level of emotional intimacy with them.

And who has the best chance of getting too close and tapping into our hurts? *Our spouses, children, families, and closest friends.*

As we distance ourselves from those who love us the most, we're essentially pushing out or separating ourselves from the most precious, God-sent gifts in our lives, and doing so in clear conflict with Christ's teaching.[79] Replacing our emptiness with authenticity can only come through exposing, closing, and dealing with the consequences of our own avoidance behaviors—which those who love us can initiate best. However, we'd perversely rather continue to wallow in our growing addictions to whatever forms of medication we've chosen to fill our holes with, despite the reality that each of these can introduce damaging consequences into our lives.

So think about it this way—our unwillingness to become more aware of our full range of feelings and face them often drives us to irrational behavior:

> *We push out the best possible influences in our lives, while*
> *potentially allowing bad influences in through self-medication.*

Jesus points out a disturbing illustration of this dynamic in Matthew 19:8, where he notes that Moses allowed divorce because of the people's hardened hearts. Divorce is clearly one of the most traumatic experiences a family can ever go through, so why wouldn't we do everything we possibly could to remove this hardening? Since hardening can be asserted to be a lack of empathy, which itself comes from a refusal or perceived inability to process and learn from difficulties, it is frustrating that when a loved one cannot or will not climb out of a self-centered state of avoidance.

This is clearly an unproductive manner of living. So what are we to do?

We must allow ourselves to *feel* who we really are. As one source pleads, "Choose to feel—(instead of) things that would keep me from feeling—alcohol to deaden emotional pain; fat-laden food to alleviate feelings of emptiness, luxury cars and other expensive items to lessen feelings of worthlessness."[80] Metaphorically, we must replant our hearts in better soil,[81] so his word and work can grow more abundantly within each of us.

You might rightly assert, "Easier said than done!"

Fortunately, through an innovative set of field research carried out with Dr. Gary Gemmill of Syracuse University, a world-renowned expert on the psychodynamics and theory of groups, and related applied research, we have found that it is not only possible, but very practical, to reverse this self-defeating pattern of avoidance and self-medication. Productively transforming our internal blueprint from evasion into real inner authenticity and growth can indeed—sometimes very quickly—establish or reestablish the passion, creativity, and wholeness in our walk with Jesus Christ.

Scripture refers to this type of transformation[82] by using the Greek word *meta-morphoo*, which is the same word used to describe Jesus' transfiguration in Matthew 17:2. Our transformation is not ordinary—it is a radical makeover!

How to achieve this transformation is the subject of the remainder of this book.

Chapter Endnotes

[44] *Men of Integrity 10 No.2 (9 March 2007).*

[45] Isaiah 9:2–7.

[46] 1 John 1:8.

[47] Romans 7:15, 18.

[48] Galatians 5:22–23.

[49] Psalms 51:6 (NLT).

[50] Romans 12:9 (KJV).

[51] *The American Heritage Dictionary of the English Language,* Fourth Edition (Houghton Mifflin, 2000), http://www.bartleby.com/61/94/D0289400.html (accessed 23 October 2006).

[52] 2 Corinthians 1:3–7.

[53] Isaiah 53:10.

[54] 1 Peter 4:10–11; Matthew 5:16.

[55] Genesis 3:7–11.

[56] Exodus 20:3–5.

[57] Ephesians 5:18.

[58] Loren (not his real name), as quoted in the *Austin American-Statesman,* 31 July 2005, page A13.

[59] Titus 2:11–12.

[60] 1 Corinthians 6:19–20, 1 Corinthians 11:20–21.

[61] Proverbs 11:13, 16:28, 20:19, 26:20, 26:22.

[62] Proverbs 29:11.

[63] Genesis 1:26–27, Psalms 8:5, Psalms 103:11–12.

[64] 2 Samuel 12:5.

[65] Robert S. McGee, *The Search for Significance* (Nashville: W Publishing Group, 2003), p.150–151.

[66] McGee, p.150–151; Job 31:33–34.

[67] Isaiah 30:9–11, 15–17.

[68] Jeremiah 6:14; James 4:17; Luke 24:13–24.

[69] William Romanowski, *Eyes Wide Open* (Grand Rapids, Michigan: Brazos Press, 2001), p.12.

[70] Exodus 16:27; Ecclesiastes 2; Luke 10:40–42.

[71] Romans 10:9.

[72] Matthew 6:1–4.

[73] 1 Samuel 3; Ephesians 5:25.

[74] Matthew 20:1–16.

[75] See http://alpha.org/

[76] Philippians 2:5–11; Philippians 4:8–10.

[77] *After Gastric Bypass Surgery, Women Battle Alcoholism,* http://abcnews.go.com/GMA/story?id=2210783&page=1&gma=true (accessed 27 August 2006).

[78] John 4:16–19; *Our Daily Bread* 50, no. 7 (15 October 2006).

[79] Matthew 19:6.

[80] *Our Daily Bread* 49, no. 10 (12 January 2005).

[81] Luke 8:5–8.

[82] 2 Corinthians 3:18.

4

An Unfortunate Skill

Then the man who had received the one talent came. "Master," he said, "I was afraid and went out and hid your talent in the ground." His Master replied, "You wicked, lazy servant! Take the talent from him and give it to the one who has the ten talents."

—*Matthew 25:24–26*

Choosing to deaden bad feelings eventually deadens our ability to feel good.

—*Our Daily Bread*[83]

As we attempt to transform our avoidance into a loving, godly witness, we will run into many challenges along the way. In this chapter, let's briefly look at the progressive degrees of *unproductive responses* to this life-changing opportunity.

These responses can be visualized by figuratively examining the amount of light that our hearts cast onto others in our lives. God commands us, as his children of light,[84] to reflect his light onto others, but our actions have the potential to veil this pure light from others. Are our hearts, through our actions, clearly reflecting his light?

In the ideal, unveiled state, others can see the light of God consistently through our actions and discussions, essentially unencumbered by self-centered or worldly diversions. Let's call this state the "unveiled heart." Godly passion, creativity, and wholeness are consistently evident, which inevitably lead to greater opportunities for those same gifts to be built up in our families, churches, ministries, friendships, and others.

We grow into this state through an emotionally intimate, personal relationship with Jesus Christ. As one commentary notes, "By gazing at the nature of God with unveiled minds, we can be more like him. In the gospel, we see the truth about Jesus Christ, and it transforms us morally as we understand and apply it. As our knowledge deepens, the Holy Spirit helps us change."[85]

Simon is a good illustration of working toward this state. After he understood how his people-pleasing behavior was alienating those closest to him—because they could never please him enough—he was able to begin turning over this familiar yet unwelcome burden to God. Then he started sharing his passion and creativity more authentically by following the plan laid out later in this book.

Unfortunately, just as we cannot maintain the unhindered level of emotional intimacy discussed earlier for an extended time, we cannot continually maintain this unveiled state of reflecting God's light. After all, Jesus Christ is the only perfect reflection of God's light.[86] Selfish desires and false underlying beliefs push us into seemingly scripted, self-centered behaviors, such as overeating, ignoring prayer, or avoiding scripture study.

Emotionally, as we choose self-medication and avoidance instead of a more authentic journey toward deeper understanding and learning, we begin to build an increasingly dense veil between ourselves and God that is analogous to the veil that hinders some from recognizing the references to Jesus in scripture.[87] As scripture states so clearly, "whenever anyone turns to the Lord, the veil is taken away."[88] We have been blessed with the ability to see and reflect his light transparently, but when we hide from our true emotions, this light becomes veiled within us, and thus hidden from our relationships.

In the first degree of unproductive response, which we'll call the "clouded heart," we're still able to relate well to others across the five levels of intimacy (acknowledgment, small talk, sharing opinions, sharing feelings, and unhindered intimacy). However, as we begin to spend discrete segments of our time managing the emotions we're not comfortable processing, we start to exhibit a subdued reflection of God's light that others can observe during these periods, where our witness seems to get lost in the crowd. At these times, we struggle to carry out Jesus's teachings to be the "salt of the earth" and the "light of the world."[89] Our unwillingness to engage with our full range of emotions begins to subtly narrow the people and places that we will engage with, as well as our openness toward authentically sharing within those confines.

Harriet is a good illustration of this stage. Her unwillingness to face inner discomfort from feeling ignored by her parents earlier in her life had resulted in this woman—who has the biggest heart in the world, according to the people who know her intimately— appearing at times as a polite lady who blends passively into the background. Her need to fortify her self-esteem through becoming a time martyr for a few codependent people was causing other people in her life to miss out on her unique gifts and ministry, which featured a deep sense of empathy and compassion across a broad range of struggles.

At first glance, one might question if we are discussing the correct issue here. If Harriet has deep empathy and compassion for others, then doesn't it make sense that she would spend most of her time with just a few folks, because this type of ministering takes time? The barometer here is Harriet herself—she talked about her immense discomfort in only ministering to the same few people over several years, as her conscience was telling her that her ministry really had a self-centered root at its core. In other words, her lack of self-awareness of what was influencing her decisions was the cloud cover over her ministry.

In the second degree of unproductive response, which we'll call the "caged heart," increasing maintenance of our emotional holes results in more substantial periods of self-focused behaviors and actions, broken only by inconsistent periods of outward compassion. Observant folks are able to see our passion, creativity, and wholeness from time to time, so they know it exists, but they get the sense that we have a lot more potential inside that seems bound up in some unexplainable way.

Victor, a health-care worker with a growing family, is a good illustration of this stage. Although having a seemingly ideal life and marriage on the surface, Victor has felt for years that his wife has been unwilling or unable to meet his emotional and physical desires. His ongoing frustration and despair have driven him into bouts with alcohol and pornography, during which times his Christian witness disappears. When Victor is not stuck in avoidance behaviors, he shows impressive initiative and leadership in the church, but because he is predictably unpredictable, his ministering even during healthy times suffers because people wonder when he will disappear again.

In the third degree of unproductive response, which we'll call the "confined heart," the self-medicating behavior essentially becomes an addiction. The light that others see through us is more like solitary confinement in a prison; some may recall our compassion from past experiences, so they're fairly confident we have a loving heart, but they cannot remember any substantial light reflected in our walk recently. Here, relationships are typically confined to the outer bands of emotional intimacy because the time we have available to share with others is consumed by habitual, self-medicating behaviors.

Matt (introduced in the "God's Intention" chapter) is a good example of this stage. Despite being known as a prominent, longtime member of a large congregation, Matt's witness has seemingly become permanently subdued, as he constantly struggles to process the anger that covers over sadness he experienced from being picked on "unmercifully" in his formative years.

Finally, if we succumb to whatever we're using to shield ourselves from our disowned emotions, then our witness becomes like a black hole—no light seems to come out, and no light appears to go in. In a way, we live as if we've had an emotional heart attack—hardened,[90] lifeless, and dead in terms of emotional intimacy. We might look like a dedicated Christian socially, but even the love that we offer others seems mechanical, done out of duty or ritual, instead of gratitude. In this fourth and final progressive degree of unproductive response, which we'll call the "black hole," true passion, wholeness, and creativity become fantasies that we simply cannot relate to.

Martha is an example of this fourth stage. Her frantic efforts to serve are readily seen by others as being robotic. As she senses others' resulting lack of affirmation toward her, she redoubles her efforts to show them that she is a good person … and the cycle continues over and over. Martha is simply trying to avoid acknowledging the intense emptiness she feels from being essentially abandoned by her parents at a young age, yet she refuses to allow herself to feel this pain. She just keeps running in circles, wondering why her church and home are "full of such ungrateful human beings."

As we advance into these deeper degrees of unproductive responses, we become increasingly incapable of authentically responding to opportunities to share God's light with the people he places in our lives. For example, when a fellow brother or sister in Christ needs to be confronted with some sin, instead of lovingly sharing God's redemptive approach in scripture,[91] we may shrink back from doing so because we fear that our own shortcomings might be attacked in retaliation. Sometimes we choose a route that is just as unacceptable and attempt to solve the problem indirectly by trying to manipulate social situations in the hope that someone else will publicly confront the offender.

Skilled Incompetence

Our inability to respond authentically to opportunities to share God's light directly parallel the conclusion that Chris Argyris, renowned organizational behavior researcher and author from Harvard University, draws from his study of how people operate in business. We can all learn much from Argyris's findings as they apply to our Christian walk.

Argyris asserts that most people operate under the same basic philosophy, which he terms the *Model I theory-in-use*:

1. We want to be in control of something.

2. We want to win.

3. We want to avoid upsetting others.[92]

Simple observation of behaviors in the corporate workplace bear out the predominance of this model. Because everyone wants to be in control of something, enterprising leaders will find a "mission" that they can own—whether or not that task is urgently needed for the success of the business over the long run. Over time, organizations predictably expand the resources supporting these missions, including a growing infrastructure of administrative staff and support functions. Then, because they all want to win, each leader sets attainable measurements and metrics that they're confident they can hit, regardless if those measurements optimally impact the firm's bottom-line performance. Then, because they want to avoid offending others, while paradoxically remaining *in control* and meeting their individual metrics, they try to stay out of everyone's way, not rock the boat, and just tend to their own moat-protected "kingdoms."

The point here is not to say that all of these missions and functions are not needed; it's just that some are overstaffed or living beyond the lifecycle of the need that gave birth to them, often while other investment-hungry business lines struggle to gather enough resources to move the firm forward more aggressively.

For example, in the mid-1990s, a leading technology firm lacked compelling solutions for an important software technology market. An industrious executive persuaded the organization to staff a spin-control team to assert publicly that this firm really was a leader in this area, despite only possessing a disparate set of uncoordinated investments across several business units. After several years, this marketing group reached more than forty employees, with a budget in the millions of dollars. The group developed increasingly grandiose and costly marketing plans, including a sponsorship for almost a million dollars of a high-profile reception at an industry trade conference—instead of focusing the investment on real products to fulfill actual needs.

Eventually, a newly appointed executive saw through this, downsized the marketing group, and turned the attention toward product acquisition and innovation. The firm became number one in that market several years later.

Although this might not sound like a big problem, what Argyris notes—and experience bears out—is that this behavior has incredibly negative effects as it pervades an organization. This model encourages each group to keep its head down and singularly focus on meeting its respective metrics, so when the business is presented with a new opportunity that would require collaboration across units, the organization on the whole is unable to respond effectively.

The net result of this behavioral model is that innovation and execution are tempered down to the point of paralysis. The organization simply cannot effectively respond to new opportunities that don't fit neatly into its existing functional tasks. Argyris starkly calls this *incompetence,* "in the sense that they produce [an outcome that] they do not intend, and they do so repeatedly, even though no one is forcing them to do so."[93] Because the organization actually becomes skilled at executing this dysfunctional model, he terms this *skilled incompetence.*

Does this model apply to our behaviors as Christians? Of course it can, given the reality of our sinful desires and nature.

We have the natural tendency to feel like we (instead of God) are (or need to be) in control of something, and we often try to apply this belief against our spouses, children, families, or friends. Then, because we want to win, we sometimes set personal goals such as whether others see our family as successful (for example, by appearing to be happy all of the time or driving the latest new car), and base our investments of time and money on maintaining that image with our neighbors, fellow churchgoers, and even ourselves—regardless of the cost. Then, because we don't want to break from societal norms or let anyone get close enough to see through our fabricated image, we limit how deep we'll let people into our lives.

Emotionally, we are naturally inclined to try to reign in the complex collection of emotions in our hearts and follow the social norm that a successful person is "always happy and in control of their emotions," while not offending anyone by "losing control" through expressing or even feeling disturbing emotions, despite their presence in us.

Our Entitlement?

An even more worrisome observation comes when we see people attempt not only to control their own emotions, but also manipulate others' as a diversion. Embracing the worldly belief that we are *entitled* to be happy all of the time is one reason that people adopt this behavior. This perceived entitlement encourages us to treat our inability to acknowledge and express our deeper troubled emotions as a topic to be avoided, aside from projecting them onto others or rationalizing them away.

This type of activity is a form of the hardening that scripture warns us about.[94] When our hearts become hardened, we in essence exclaim that we'll "run our own ship" and lose faith that God can deliver us from, and teach us through, the emotional pain in our lives. In Ephesians, scripture explains that hardening leads to ignorance and insensitivity,[95] which obviously drives both personal and inter-personal problems.

The fundamental problem here is that worldly happiness—the subject of our perceived entitlement—is a temporary emotional state. A sense of entitlement causes us to strive for affirmation and meaning through the temporal fruit of the world instead of driving toward authenticity through God's eternal fruit.[96] What is the difference? Let's look at the radical differences between the temporal or worldly fruit versus God's spiritual fruit:

	Godly fruit	**Worldly fruit**
Source	Our all-powerful God's Holy Spirit (Galatians 5:22)	The extremely limited power of our innately sinful nature
Motiva-tion	To be in relationship with God and live out his call to love one another compassionately (Matthew 22:37–40)	To satisfy a desire for or feeling of entitlement to greater material attainment and comfort for self
Goals	To expand God's kingdom (Matthew 28:19)	To expand my personal kingdom
Peace	Lasting, confident assurance that God is in control in all circumstances (Philippians 4:6, 7)	A temporary state of good feelings, positive thinking, absence of conflict, or a combination of these
Love	Choosing to share our unique God-given gifts patiently, humbly, and compassionately (1 Corinthians 13)	Self-seeking desire, pleasure and lust
Joy	Deep, lasting awe based on the wonder of God's creation, grace, and mercy (John 16:21)	Temporary happiness that stems from worldly achievement, idolatrous acquisition, and/or pleasant circumstances
Patience	Resting in the comfort and perspective of our eternal life with God (1 Timothy 1:16)	Desiring immediate personal gratification
Kind-ness	Heart-felt giving that leads us and others toward reconciliation with God and each other (Romans 2:4)	Being nice to manipulate others for selfish gain or to build up one's self-esteem
Good-ness	Fighting through our sinful desires to take the morally correct path (Romans 5:8b)	Doing good things to manipulate others for selfish gain or in an attempt to build self-worth
Faithful-ness	Not compromising our belief and trust in the one true God (Daniel 3)	Supporting people or causes until a more attractive or fulfilling offer comes along
Gentle-ness	Humility that stems from accepting his grace and mercy, which he shares with us despite our sinfulness (Matthew 5:5)	Holding one's gifts back because of a lack of self-esteem or faking "gentle Christian" manners to look good to others
Self-Control	Holding onto faith with a clear conscience by not yielding to worldly temptation (1 Timothy 1:19)	Temporarily resisting temptation until we think no one is looking or we can't hold out any longer

Figure 3: Contrasting Godly and Worldly Fruit

Embracing Our Emotions

The point here is that not only do we naturally struggle with owning the uncomfortable emotions within us, but the behavioral philosophy that we sometimes operate under causes us to become *skilled at being incompetent* in facing up to these! In other words, we settle for a short-term gain because the relatively small but immediate cost of avoidance allows us to perceive that we're winning, in control, and not upsetting anyone, which makes it far easier to continue compromising as we strive for the eternal gifts that God has in store for us.

This unproductive model of processing our emotions leads to observable hypocrisy in our Christian walk. Although we may be able to talk a good talk—telling friends that we'll pray for their problems, listening to Christian music in our cars, and maybe even quoting our favorite scripture from time to time—we're unable to convert this into consistent compassionate outreach because our emotional ineffectiveness prevents us from overcoming the barriers to more authenticity in our walk.

And because this reality limits our ability to be blessed with God's spiritual fruit, we will be more easily diverted by the temporary worldly feelings that we define as our personal success factors. "I'm not happy today," we figuratively or literally exclaim, "and you're the reason, so either you shape up or there's going to be trouble." This, of course, likely evokes a defensive reaction in our spouse, child, friend, colleague, or family member, which leads to all sorts of unproductive outcomes.

We must embrace all of our emotions. Analogous to scripture's description of our physical bodies,[97] we're made up of many emotions—some strong, some weak, some honorable, some less honorable, and even some that are unpresentable without a proper level of modesty. But we must accept all of them to fully realize the open hearts that God's law commands us to pursue.[98] God's word should inspire us to be bighearted people with an expanding ability to appreciate him and others, regardless of differences that appear on the surface, because of our growing understanding of the similar issues that so many of us share!

Gifts and Talents

It may sound strange to call the experiences, even the painful ones, that lead to the intense emotions that we try to avoid owning as *gifts*, but that's exactly what they are. Brother Andre, a French Canadian monastic, observes that "if we knew the value of suffering, we would ask for it."[99] Another insightful source states,

"Few unbroken lives in this world are useful to God. But man's disappointments are often God's appointments, and the things we believe are tragedies may be the very opportunities through which God chooses to exhibit his love and grace. For a Christian, wholeness always comes after brokenness."[100] Scripture says, "It was good for me to be afflicted so that I might learn your decrees."[101]

Growing from and sharing these unique gifts can have a substantial impact on how our walk affects others' understanding of Jesus Christ, as Paul points out to the church at Corinth.[102] Scripture notes that we're to "ensure hardship as discipline ... strengthen your feeble arms and weak knees. Make level paths for your feet, so that the lame may not be disabled, but rather healed."[103] In other words, as we work through our issues and our Christian witness becomes more consistent, then others will be able to follow more effectively behind our experience and witness. This also helps us personally grow. As Dr. Gary Gemmill notes, "As you love others, you love yourself also."

These gifts are opportunities to learn, a form of "hidden manna,"[104] so we can grow in our empathy and love for others. Just as a beautiful pearl begins to grow from an oyster's open wound, our bright witness for Christ can begin to grow out of our emotional wounds.

Taking this concept even further, we can think about our uncomfortable experiences and emotions as talents—powerful opportunities[105] to share his light effectively.[106] And Jesus expects us to use these talents, as discussed in the parable of the same name.[107] But when we do not learn from these gifts, and rather embark on a life of denial and emotional ineffectiveness, God's light becomes veiled. If we just bury these gifts, we shouldn't be surprised when God does not—*cannot*—bless us with even more, because we haven't learned from that which he's blessed us with already!

Choosing to bury these emotional gifts instead of learning from them mimics the typical human reaction to God's other blessings for us as well. Whether intellectual, physical, spiritual, or emotional, we generally adopt one of three attitudes toward our gifts:

1. *Complacency.* We take our God-given gifts for granted and consider our possession of them as something to be pridefully protected. Here, there is little to no desire to share these gifts with others unless we can realize some self-centered gain.

2. *Rebellion.* We dismiss our God-given gifts as either inadequate or worthless and spend our time pursuing the attractive gifts that we see God has blessed others with. Scripture clearly condemns coveting what is not

ours, whether an influential position, a certain spiritual gift, a friend's attractive spouse, a fancy automobile, musical talent, or anything else.[108] A particular emotional gift that so many rebelliously pursue is the perception that God has blessed a specific person or group of people with happiness through a distinct level of worldly attainment, which encourages a belief that they too will be happy if they can attain that same level.

3. *Contentment.* We accept the gifts that God has uniquely blessed us with and use them to love God and others humbly. Obviously, this is the attitude that scripture implores us to follow.[109] While both complacency and rebellion lead us into unproductive behaviors that make it nearly impossible to follow the scriptural command to "make the most of every opportunity,"[110] contentment enables us to perform authentic godly service.

Ultimately, when we do not embrace all of our emotions, we essentially create and hold onto burdens that we don't need to carry—a burden of maintaining a false mask that requires a tremendous amount of energy. This dynamic brings to mind the fascinating story of the Franklin Expedition in the mid-1800s, which was attempting to find a path from the United Kingdom across the Arctic Ocean.[111]

Both of the expedition's ships had been overpacked with worthless, ornate treasures—more than one thousand books, silverware engraved with officers' initials, and even fine china—yet underpacked with fuel. After getting trapped in stronger ice floes than expected, and after many deaths, several groups of sailors decided to try to cross the ice to safety. Sadly, two officers who were found dead after traveling more than sixty-five miles had been *pulling a sled full of engraved silverware.*

What useless burdens are you still pulling along, hidden away in your heart?

Chapter Endnotes

[83] *Our Daily Bread* 49, no. 10 (12 January 2005).

[84] John 12:36.

[85] Life Application Bible, New International Version, (Grand Rapids, MI: Zondervan, 1991). Study note from 2 Corinthians 3:18, copyright 1986, owned by assignment by Tyndale House Publishers, Inc.

[86] Colossians 1:15.

[87] This veil was symbolically ripped away as the Temple curtain fell at the conclusion of Jesus Christ's crucifixion, as noted in Luke 23:45b.

[88] 2 Corinthians 3:16.

[89] Matthew 5:13–16.

[90] Psalms 95:8.

[91] Matthew 18:15–17.

[92] Argyris, Chris, *Overcoming Organizational Defenses: Facilitating Organizational Learning* (Needham Heights, MA: Allyn and Bacon, 1990), p. 13.

[93] Argyris, p. 14.

[94] Psalms 95:8.

[95] Ephesians 4:18–19.

[96] Such as that described in Ephesians 5:18.

[97] 1 Corinthians 12:14–26.

[98] Psalms 119:32 (KJV).

[99] *Men of Integrity* 7, no. 6 (17 December 2004).

[100] *Our Daily Bread* 50, no. 1 (1 April 2005).

[101] Psalms 119:71.

[102] 2 Corinthians 1:7–11.

[103] Hebrews 12:7, 12–13.

[104] Revelation 2:17.

[105] 1 Timothy 4:4, 5.

[106] Matthew 5:13–16.

[107] Matthew 25:14–30.

[108] Exodus 20:17.

[109] Luke 3:14; Philippians 4:11–12; 1 Timothy 6:8; Hebrews 13:5.

[110] Colossians 4:5.

[111] *Our Daily Bread* 50, no. 4 (2 July 2005).

5

Building Emotional Authenticity—A Plan

The Lord gives sight to the blind.

—*Psalm 146:8a*

I can do everything through him who gives me strength.

—*Philippians 4:13*

… they might see with their eyes,
hear with their ears,
understand with their hearts,
and turn and be healed.

—*Isaiah 6:10*

One-half of knowing what you want
is knowing what you must give up before you get it.

—*Sidney Howard, playwright*[112]

It's time to remove these burdens—the hidden barriers in your walk with Jesus Christ that you've unknowingly held onto for years, decades, or maybe even a lifetime. In our research, we have worked with hundreds of people, many who have built layer upon layer of defense in an ongoing quest to avoid the pain caused by the very experiences that God intends to be learning experiences.

The result of building these barriers is always the same: we transform a temporal pain that was intended to guide us toward godly wisdom, praise, and lasting appreciation into an ever-present thorn that lies waiting to torment those introspective moments when the noise and busyness of our lives take an unsolicited break.

Jesus intends for us to learn from these pains, which essentially form an emotional cross—perhaps part of what he had in mind when he commanded us to pick up and carry our own cross.[113] And he is not going to give up on us. He knows the barriers we erect and waits patiently for us to wholeheartedly accept the instruction he wants us to receive.[114] As scripture states, "Here I am! I stand at the door and knock. If anyone hears my voice and opens the door, I will come in and eat with him, and he with me."[115]

> God has the power to free you from your pain.
> God has the power to tear down the self-imposed barriers
> that are hindering your Christian walk.

> God *wants* you to enjoy his spiritual fruit,
> which will replenish your natural fuel
> for compassionately serving him out of gratitude
> through living out his divine plan.

Analogous to Jesus departing his earthly tomb for our salvation,[116] we must bravely depart our emotional tombs to grow closer to him and his people. As the psalmist states, "Search me, O God, and know my heart; test me and know my anxious thoughts. See if there is any offensive way in me, and lead me in the way everlasting."[117] How do we effectively follow God here? The biblical account of original sin[118] gives us a good example of what *not* to do:

Ineffective witness	*Effective witness*
Adam and Eve took action based on the belief that their way was superior to God's way.	We should take action based on the knowledge that God's plan for us, including the pain that we've experienced, is superior to our desire for temporary worldly fruit.
After realizing their sin, Adam and Eve felt convicted and tried to hide what God already knew.	We should be open to see within ourselves what is already obvious to God because he gives us the strength to do so.
Adam and Eve tried to rationalize away their sin to God.	We should take responsibility for what is in our hearts and ask God for help with it.

Figure 4: How to Follow God Toward Emotional Authenticity

Scripture urges us to give up the deception of self-medication when it states that we're to "be clear minded and self-controlled so that you can pray (and) love each other deeply."[119] But no one can force you to embark on this truly courageous journey of learning from your unique experiences and challenges. Your spouse cannot. Your pastor cannot. This book certainly cannot. And Jesus Christ *will not* because he loves you too much to take away your free will to choose emotional authenticity.

An Old Testament prophet exclaimed God's word in the following way: "I will lead the blind by ways they have not known, along unfamiliar paths I will guide them; I will turn the darkness into light before them and make the rough places smooth."[120] In the New Testament, Paul notes simply that "A man ought to examine himself."[121] Why? Because it opens us up to *a fundamentally greater degree of authentic godly fruit through the elimination of the emptiness in our hearts caused by self-medication and avoidance.* In truth, our deepest, most uncomfortable emotions provide us with some of the greatest opportunities to grow closer to him!

A mineworker living under the brutal regime of Kim Jung II in North Korea was quoted as saying that "a full heart comes with a full stomach."[122] In the developed world, we have all of the resources one could ask for, so what's our excuse for not pursuing the authenticity of a heart full of empathetic compassion?

If *your* heart is willing, even just ever so slightly, then please read on …

The most fundamental reality that you must accept about this plan is that *building emotional authenticity is an ongoing process, not a destination.* It is a course of action that leads to increasingly "juicy" levels of godly fruit as he guides you to understand and remove the impurities from your walk.[123]

Please be careful to not short-circuit this process as you enter into it. Taking the easy route is encouraged by two of today's more alluring yet perilous values:

- The worldly value of *immediate gratification* will entice you to try to rush through the process when you begin to recognize your self-medicative habits and underlying issues for the first time. Although you may be tempted to deal with the issues, get "fixed," and move on, doing so typically leads to only surface-level treatment of deeper wounds and little inner authenticity.

  It is important to note, however, that the process of building emotional authenticity is *not* based on perpetually wallowing in the same pain.

Although it only takes a moment of faith to be born again, authenticity is a lifelong process that consists of progressively and constructively exposing and eliminating the defensive barriers and self-defeating scripts that you've built over your lifetime. You must continually grow in your understanding of how God is shaping you through your challenges as he decreases your focus on worldly destinations and goals.

- As stated earlier, the worldly value of *entitlement* may encourage you to turn toward seeking temporal happiness as you recognize the depth of the awareness and understanding you must achieve. Individually, people sometimes seek happiness through subtly "trading up" to another form of self-medication. Communally, be careful that you do not promote a worldly sense of entitlement in your church that "if you're holy then you'll always be happy," or you may be contributing to a much broader authenticity problem. As Larry Crabb critiques, "the experience of groaning is precisely what modern Christianity so often tries to help us escape."[124] Remember, emotional authenticity is not some mythical state of being happy all of the time. Yearning for this imaginary ideal may be a major influence that has been leading you into self-medication and avoidance!

Instead, you must stick with two basic principles throughout this ongoing process to be ultimately successful:

1. You must be *willing to admit* your chosen form(s) of self-medication, and

2. You must be *willing to face* the underlying emotional pain that led you to self-medicate.

As you follow these principles, you will reach numerous milestones in your quest for greater authenticity. How can you tell when you've reached such a landmark? You'll recognize it when you understand how dealing with a specific emotional issue has led to a positive difference in how you experience yourself and others. This often is characterized by the following:

- *Empathy.* You can now truly relate to someone whom you have not been able to relate to before, making it possible to love them (and others like them) more compassionately. Dennis De Haan wrote a beautiful poem that reflects this sentiment:

> If you once bore a heavy load
> That drove you to despair

You'll have a heart for those who bend
Beneath their load of care.[125]

- *Gratitude.* You can now more discernibly appreciate specific gifts that God has blessed you with, instead of looking at them as unwelcome burdens. Your shift in attitude enables you to share your gifts with others more generously. For example, as Harriet (introduced earlier) processed the root pain of her "time martyr" form of self-medication, she came to understand that the deep compassion she has for others is a priceless gift when shared properly. This stood out in stark contrast to the many years when this gift felt more like an affliction to her as she primarily shared it with her few codependent friends in a recurring attempt to affirm her self-worth.

- *Understanding.* You can more confidently recognize and cut through the internal defenses that have been holding back your witness with certain people and situations, allowing you to be more responsive to God's call and people with your gifts. For example, as Simon (introduced earlier) processed the root pain underlying his people-pleasing behavior, he realized he had essentially written off his wife emotionally because of her unwillingness to provide him with a constant "fix" of affirmation. This enabled him to focus on sincerely listening to and investing in his wife—her desires, thoughts, and challenges—thus building a far deeper connection within their marriage.

- *Freedom.* You are now less emotionally constrained by self-medicating activities, allowing you to share your unique set of God-given gifts with others more consistently and authentically.

The Emotional Authenticity Cycle

Now, for the process itself.

The process of building emotional authenticity takes place through a repeating cycle of four stages, which I term the *emotional authenticity cycle.*

Let's look at each stage in detail, based on the simple reality that *the hidden barriers to more passion, creativity, and wholeness in your walk are constructed of emotional issues that you have avoided discussing or have disowned, along with the self-medications that prevent you from either discussing or owning them.* In other words, we'll examine those things that prevent you from picking up your emotional cross and moving forward.

In the first stage, you must prepare yourself to be able to discuss and take ownership of your root issues. To accomplish this, you must take a strong and courageous[126] step:

STAGE ONE: Identify and begin to wean off your chosen form(s) of self-medication.

You can look at this first stage figuratively in terms of your physical body. If you continually put unhealthy foods and other substances in your body, then unhealthy toxins and fat will begin to build. Despite God blessing you with a miraculous physical body that normally does everything it can to keep itself functioning properly, eventually it will break down, and disease or death will result. However, if you stop pouring in unhealthy substances, your body will usually cleanse itself naturally.

Similarly, in terms of your emotions, you must wean yourself off of whatever form(s) of toxic self-medication you've become attached or addicted to. To do this, you must be willing to identify what form(s) you rely on, as well as be open to recognizing the impact that this misconsumption is having across your life—with your family, friends, co-workers, and even within yourself.

Are you available for others when they need you most? Are you truly there, fully engaged, in the moment, in heart, body, and mind? Or are you frequently changing the scenery (people and places) in your life, like some tried to do in the Old Testament, hoping that this change will somehow alter the way you ultimately feel?[127]

The opportunity cost of self-medication is enormous. Every moment that you spend self-medicating, or dealing with the aftereffects of it on yourself and others, is a moment that you're not available to serve with more authentic compassion the people God is sending into your life.

Some might assert that "beginning to wean off" of our chosen form(s) of self-medication is not enough—that we must go "cold turkey" to truly have an impact. Our research shows that this is not true.

In Simon's case, during his workaholic phase, he began to slowly wean himself away from the office by coming home early just one or two afternoons each week. After a few weeks, he reported being pleasantly surprised at how quickly he was able to sense the relationships he had been missing at home, which then of course fueled even further progress.

Notice that self-medicating against your emotional reality is ironically similar to many physical medications—its effects last only a short time, and an increasing amount is often required to get the same benefit. And in this case, "benefit" is a suspect term to use, because we're talking about *a temporary break from reality that is accompanied by an opportunity cost for your personal ministry.*

How have others effectively implemented this first stage? Here are some constructive observations from our research.

- If you self-medicate by strictly adhering to some set of godly or secular laws, then allow yourself to think about how tough it is to show God's grace and mercy humbly to those who you feel are less law abiding than you. There's an old saying that when you're driving on a highway, everyone going faster than you seems like a maniac, and everyone going slower seems like an idiot. Relying on adherence to law causes us to treat others similarly—that is, judgmentally—which creates a hypocritical Christian witness. Do *you* reach out to others lovingly, without the faintest hint of superiority in your attitude? Remember that Jesus lovingly reached out to all sinners, from tax collectors to adulterers.[128] Recognize any personal hypocrisy here by reading and meditating on relevant scripture, such as Jesus's story about the Samaritan helping the beaten man in Luke 10:30–37, where the priest was unwilling to help because of compliance with purification laws. Or, read and meditate on Romans 3:27, Matthew 3:8–9, or even Jesus's strong words to the Pharisees in Matthew 23, where their very public adherence to hundreds of laws was at odds with the sin in their hearts.

- If you self-medicate through one of the more socially approved forms, such as work or ministry, then allow yourself to observe and record each time that you're not there mentally, in the moment of need, for those whom God has sent your way. This can include time when you're "stuck" in the office or at church, as well as the time you spend at home worrying about these, while your family wonders what planet you've mentally wandered off to. Begin to create a more sensible balance by giving up the unrealistic responsibility for solving every problem (yours and everyone else's), answering every e-mail, catching every call—essentially trying to keep everyone impressed or happy all of the time. Many time-management programs can assist here, but please remember that the goal is not to figure out how to stuff more work or ministry into your existing schedule. Your goal is to figure out how to include these responsibilities within a life that properly places God and family ahead of them.

- If you self-medicate through any of the other common methods, then allow yourself to see the true extent of the time that you spend diverting yourself and dealing with the consequences, instead of properly sharing your unique gifts. And please remember, once again, to avoid simply "trading up" to more socially respected patterns of self-medication!

After starting this process toward greater authenticity, you will be able to see how self-medication has perverted your priorities and how disorder results when you don't put God and family first. If this is the state you're in, then you can start developing your authenticity by substituting family and spiritual activities that allow you to share your gifts. For example, in Simon's case, instead of spending his evening hours at work and ministry, he used the time to share in his children's schoolwork, playtime, and hobbies.

Please also note that as you begin this process toward greater authenticity, you're still going to be tempted by your chosen form(s) of self-medication, possibly to excruciating levels. As Mart De Haan boldly exclaims, "Coming to the end of yourself emotionally could be the most painful experience you've ever encountered."[129] Satan does not give up his hold on us easily. He will try to convince you that the temporary fix of avoidance is far better than any touchy-feely, namby-pamby connectedness you could eventually experience, especially because the pain that your self-medication temporarily hides is likely to emerge more than once throughout this process.

Satan relies on you keeping your root issues hidden, and he feeds on these just as some animals feed on grubs buried in the ground. He tries to convince you (or keep you convinced) that you don't deserve to feel authentic peace and joy; that you'll never fully measure up; that fate really is against you; that you deserve the shame, sadness, or guilt you feel; that anyone who tries to tell you different is a dreamer.

This kind of internal talk has attracted you to your chosen form(s) of self-medication for so long because no one *wants* to listen to these familiar kinds of accusations. But you must! Face the chatter now. As the psalmist bravely asks, "Why are you downcast, O my soul? Why so disturbed within me?"[130] Allow yourself to connect more deeply with what you really feel inside today, regardless of how difficult or discouraging it may seem at first.

And then continue to the second stage:

STAGE TWO: Pick up your emotional cross.

To do this, you will first need to understand what your emotional cross actually looks like. This means you must take the painful experiences and feelings that you've been unable to talk about (which, ironically is a fact that is often itself undiscussable), and learn to talk about them. *Discuss the undiscussable.*

How exactly do you make the "undiscussable" discussable? You don't rational-ize your chosen form(s) of self-medication with others. Nor do you chat endlessly about the effects that this self-medication has had on those you love and others who are in your life. Although these topics are important points along the road to recovery, they are not the ultimate target. The ultimate goal is discovering the root emotion(s) that you've disowned because these hold the real key to discover-ing your more authentic heart. Finding your authenticity will enable God's love to shine with greater brightness through you to the others in your life.

If you can feel it, God can heal it. How do you discover your hidden emotional roots? By being brave and wise enough to get help.

You must have the humility and courage to admit that you need help and can-not do it on your own. God either has, or will, put empathetic people in your life—friends, family, and acquaintances—who can truly understand what you're going through. As you courageously open yourself to become aware of and understand their similar experiences, you will be increasingly emboldened to face your toughest issues—often with their compassionate support.

On some occasions, compassionate help from peers will not be able to help you sufficiently process your issues. In this case, professional help is the answer. Whether you choose group counseling, individual counseling, or some other pro-gram, many types of professionals are trained to help you start where you are and guide you—only as you permit—to your previously hidden emotions. And you'll realize not only that going there doesn't kill you, but also that it gives you the freedom to no longer be enslaved to your chosen form(s) of self-medication and its related negative effects.

Society has influenced some people to believe that participating in professional counseling is an admission of failure, an embarrassment to be hidden from oth-ers. This is a huge fallacy that must be let go:

- You consult with a medical doctor for a physical ailment, or you may stray from physical health.

- You consult with a teacher for an intellectual void, or you may stray from academic enlightenment.

- You consult with a pastor for a spiritual ailment, or you may stray from godly wisdom.

- You consult with a professional counselor for an emotional ailment, or you may stray from emotional authenticity.

God blesses these professionals with their gifts, so it is unwise to not learn from their understanding and wisdom!

Another important reason to seek professional help when needed is because when you start to adopt this cycle, you may not be prepared to delve as deeply as you may need to in order to fully work through your internal struggles. Some people are able to dive head first into this work, but others can take a longer time to reach a similar depth of awareness and understanding. There is no right amount of time to gain understanding; it occurs as one is willing and able to go deeper. Professionals are trained on these dynamics and can properly support your unique journey.

Regardless of how long it takes to make progress, we all have a responsibility to pursue our hidden roots. Scripture tells us that we must discover what within us is causing us to sin,[131] and the self-medicative habits we use to attempt to hide our emotional roots certainly can fall into this category.

This describes the emotional cross that we must pick up. The cross is symbolic of our continuing struggle to become more holy in a secular world. This struggle leads to our instruction and spiritual evolution—if we are wise enough to choose this path.

God has blessed you with a unique set of gifts to authentically carry out his divine plan. Because he has *already* sent his only Son to die on the cross to pay for your sins, and has *already* resurrected his only Son to defeat evil and death for you, and has *already* sent his Holy Spirit to be your counselor to provide the godly fruit that feeds your walk with him, you have a duty to fulfill his plan—but he does not force you to do so.

You may have to contend with two final rationalizations before you give yourself permission to face your hidden emotional roots. You may exclaim:

- "But I'm a special case, and there's no way God can really understand *just how painful* my pain is. He really couldn't have allowed me to go through what I did, at least if he really was in control and really loved me."

- "But my problems are nothing compared to other people I know. I mean, I wasn't physically abused or anything like that! My problems aren't important enough to spend a bunch of time dealing with them."

If you can identify with either reaction, be comforted by the fact that God has always been in control and thinks highly enough of you to allow you to experience what you did. There is a reason that you endured your experience, regardless of your perception of its significance. As scripture states so clearly, "There hath no temptation taken you but such as is common to man: but God is faithful, who will not suffer you to be tempted above that ye are able; but will with the temptation make also a way to escape, that ye may be able to bear it."[132]

God knows you can handle it. And you must handle it. Because as you begin to take ownership of your true feelings and emotions, you'll begin to find yourself empowered to resist blindly projecting them onto others as you more authentically interact with others. As Benjamin Disraeli, the former British prime minister, said, "Never apologize for showing feeling. Remember that when you do, you apologize for the truth."[133] We just need to be sure to reveal our feelings constructively and lovingly.

Notice that these first two stages of the emotional authenticity cycle have an interesting parallel with the definition of love discussed earlier: "a decision and action to meet another's needs." You must *decide* to stop your self-medicating habits or addictions, and then take *action* to pick up your cross. The difference here is that you're enabling yourself to meet others' needs in the future by dealing with your own now!

As you begin to extract yourself from self-medication, and as you get assistance to work through your formerly hidden roots, you can move to the third stage:

STAGE THREE: Carry your emotional cross

What does this mean—to carry your cross? It means to move toward greater authenticity through acknowledging, appreciating, and working with your true feelings, however painful some of them may be. Needless to say, we need heaps of help from God to do this with any consistency.

How does God help us here?

Blaise Pascal once said, "There is a God-shaped vacuum in the heart of every man which cannot be filled by any created thing, but only by God, the Creator, made known through Jesus."[134] And that's our answer. God provides you with an abundance of resources and blessings that can fill in those holes in your heart so you can move into greater awareness and authenticity. He can mend the pain you've been avoiding and use that pain to make you even more dangerous to Satan. He gives you the empathy and courage to recognize these emotions in others, and then help them grow out of their own emotional bondage through your example and witness.

God will help you "turn from darkness to light."[135] He accomplishes this specifically as you more authentically engage with the people whom he's sent to you,

- Through Jesus Christ, who paid the ultimate price so you could reflect God's light

- Through the Holy Spirit, the counselor that Jesus promised, who gives you the daily support and guidance you need

- Through those who wrote God-inspired scripture to guide you toward greater faith, goodness, knowledge, self-control, perseverance, godliness, kindness, and love[136]

- Through the professional helpers and mentors that he's blessed your life with

- Through the compassionate people he's placed in your life right now, to aid you in worship, Bible study, retreats, accountability groups, service opportunities, etc.

- Through the others that he'll continue to enrich your life with, with whom you'll be able to share your increasingly authentic compassion, while discerning even more understanding from their unique journeys.

This assistance has already been at your front gate, but you may have been allowing pride and fear to keep the gates locked. Unlock those gates and take a chance!

When you do, you'll discover the astonishing amount of space that your self-medication and hidden roots have been collectively taking up in your life. Your self-medication (and its effect on both yourself and others) creates a huge opportunity cost because it results in your true gifts not being shared—an absence that clearly affects the broader Christian body.[137] And when you fear that looking at your hidden roots could incapacitate yourself or others, your fear may grow so large that you block entire groups of people, places, and feelings out of your Christian walk.

Incidentally, this third stage is an important step for breaking the "skilled incompetence" dynamic discussed in a previous chapter. For businesses, Chris Argyris argues that successful organizations must implement a new model in which leaders are willing to face reality more bluntly, including the willingness to process distressing yet valid data, and then reset the assumptions used to evaluate success. Likewise, with respect to emotional authenticity, we must be willing to face more bluntly what is truly inside of us, and then move forward in our walk in a way that acknowledges and grows from these critical revelations, instead of continuing to hide from them.

As you immerse yourself into these opportunities with the help of his light[138]—with *your heart in his hand, instead of your head in the sand*—ultimately, his Holy Spirit will show you more and more how working through your sufferings will lead to a much stronger kingdom. And as you realize this, you can move onto the final step:

**STAGE FOUR: Reflect on your progress,
while adopting this model of increasing understanding and appreciation.**

Instead of living as a self-absorbed worldly addict, live as a humble child of God, obediently resting in an ever-increasing understanding and appreciation of yourself, others, and God's amazing grace and offer of eternal life. This latter gift keeps on giving, as it is often accompanied by the godly fruit that allows you to reach out even more authentically to those he places in your path. As you do this, you'll continue to see his gifts to you more clearly—the people, experiences, and even sufferings that he has blessed your life with to bring you closer to him—so you can more brilliantly share his light in a struggling world. You can truly, *observably* begin to carry out his divine plan more consistently in your walk.

When you adopt this model, you'll also increasingly recognize the many different emotions and feelings that your personal cross is made up of and how God miraculously forms them into something that binds you and his church together. In other words, as you understand and begin to process a newly exposed emotional root, you'll recognize related roots that you simply were not able to see before acknowledging the current one, and you'll understand how your unwillingness or inability to process these has artificially constricted your witness.

You'll also notice that this new model of living becomes especially actionable as you further embrace one of his greatest gifts of all—the opportunity for deeper study and understanding of his word. For example, God's word teaches us that we will suffer in many ways for our own good.[139] As you adopt this model, you'll see how your unique sufferings help you better understand the enormity of his grace and mercy. You begin to realize how some of the pain that you blame others for may have actually been self-inflicted—either from consequences of things you did or because of your own naïve understanding of the consequences of others' self-medication—especially relative to your relationship with your parents.

The importance of obediently learning from your sufferings is just one example of the beautiful gift that your growing emotional awareness will draw you toward—an increasing level of godly wisdom. Turning away from self-deception, and toward those to whom God has imparted compassion, knowledge, and understanding of emotional crosses like yours, will help you more obediently seek him as your spiritual, physical, intellectual, and emotional gifts are freed from the former bondage of self-medication and avoidance.

Rediscovering an Old Friend

Gaining wisdom about what pain was imposed onto us versus what pain was self-inflicted is particularly relevant for adult issues that stem from childhood. Psalm 8:2 states that children have been ordained for praise, but when adults refuse to look inside at what is sometimes termed their "inner child," it is not because they fear finding too much joyous worship there!

Children will often wrongly blame themselves for family dysfunction or damaging incidents, such as not running away from an abuser, not speaking up when being beaten by an alcoholic parent, or not being "good enough" to make one's parents "happy." These children then carry that hidden blame into adulthood, where it shows up in all sorts of self-destructive patterns. And when they then cast or project blame, they harbor resentments that shield them from the incredible power of forgiveness and unity.[140]

By adopting the four-stage cycle discussed in this chapter, these now-adult children understand not only that those childhood dysfunctions and incidents were *not* their fault, but that in many cases, the perpetrators never intentionally intended to harm them deliberately. The offenders may have been unknowingly medicating themselves against *their own* unresolved pains. As Mignon McLaughlin once said, "Most of us become parents long before we have stopped being children."[141]

Enlightened understanding such as this gives us an opportunity to eliminate the bondage of our self-disparaging scripts and underlying false beliefs that have silently ruled our lives for years, decades, or even a lifetime. This allows us to appreciate better the complex realities of interpersonal living, and then both confess to those we've wronged and forgive those who have wronged us—rather than avoid and self-medicate!

Ultimately, this new model of emotional authenticity consists of more constructively and progressively discovering and dealing with the issues that are already inside of you. The great philosopher George Santayana alluded to this well when he said, "To be interested in the changing seasons is a happier state of mind than to be hopelessly in love with spring."[142] Instead of feeling stuck living in some false mode of perceived happiness while justifying defensive actions to remove any actual or perceived threats to this happiness, you must accept the faults of yourself and others, patiently recognizing that you and they may not yet be in a place where these faults and their effects can be fully recognized and processed.

Scripture states that we will find God when we seek him with all our heart.[143] Trust that he is giving you this opportunity to work through your troubling roots in order to develop your godly witness as you become able to reach out with an increasingly authentic compassion toward those he is placing along your path.

Praise be to the Lord!

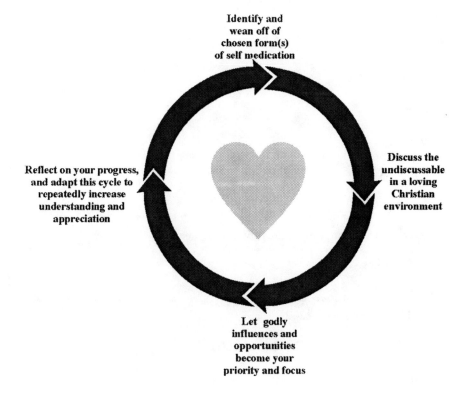

Identify and
wean off of
chosen form(s)
of self medication

Discuss the
undiscussable
in a loving
Christian
environment

Reflect on your progress,
and adapt this cycle to
repeatedly increase
understanding and
appreciation

Let godly
influences and
opportunities
become your
priority and focus

Chapter Endnotes

[112] Sidney Howard Quotes, http://www.brainyquote.com/quotes/quotes/s/sidneyhowa172311.html (accessed 6 September 2006).

[113] Luke 14:27.

[114] Isaiah 49:16; Romans 6:17.

[115] Revelation 3:20.

[116] John 20:10–18.

[117] Psalms 139:23–24.

[118] Genesis 3.

[119] 1 Peter 4:3, 7–8.

[120] Isaiah 42:16.

[121] 1 Corinthians 11:28.

[122] *Austin American-Statesman,* 24 July 2005, page H4.

[123] Ezekiel 36:25.

[124] Crabb, Larry, *Inside Out* (Colorado Springs, CO: Navpress Publishing Group, 1998); Romans 8:22–26.

[125] *Our Daily Bread* 50, no. 3 (12 June 2005).

[126] Deuteronomy 31:6.

[127] Numbers 23.

[128] Luke 19:5; John 8:3–11.

[129] *Our Daily Bread* 50, no. 4 (12 July 2005).

[130] Psalms 42:5.

[131] Matthew 5:29–30; Mark 9:43–47.

[132] 1 Corinthians 10:13 (KJV).

[133] Benjamin Disraeli Quotes, http://www.brainyquote.com/quotes/quotes/b/benjamindi104288.html (accessed 20 August 2006).

[134] Blaise Pascal Quotes, http://thinkexist.com/quotation/there_is_a_god_shaped_vacuum_in_the_heart_of/166425.html (accessed 20 August 2006).

[135] Acts 26:18.

[136] 2 Peter 1:5–9.

[137] Romans 12:4–8.

[138] John 1:5.

[139] 2 Corinthians 1:3–7 et al.

[140] Psalms 103:12.

[141] Mignon McLaughlin Quotes, http://www.brainyquote.com/quotes/authors/m/mignon_mclaughlin.html (accessed 27 August 2006).

[142] Santayana, George. http://www.quotationspage.com/quotes/George_Santayana (accessed 20 August 2006).

[143] Jeremiah 29:13.

6

Building Emotional Authenticity—Observable Fruit

Blessed are you who weep now, for you will laugh.

—*Luke 6:21b*

God's word brings health and healing to every sin-sick soul,
but we must take and heed it before we can be whole.

—*Dennis De Haan*[144]

As you adopt the emotional authenticity cycle, and as the chains begin to fall away from your walk, you may be shocked at how prominently your passion, creativity, and wholeness begin to renew daily.[145] These crucial provisions from God are *already present* inside of you. Your role is simply to embrace them—and then share them.

Passion

Your *passion* for the Lord will naturally shine through when you're sharing "all" of you, instead of some fabricated partial representation. After all, we always find time to do that which we enjoy the most, which is in its purest form when we're contentedly and compassionately sharing the gifts that God has uniquely blessed each one of us with.

Passion, which is also called fervor or enthusiasm in some translations of the Bible, is literally a scriptural command that parallels God's zeal for his creation in sacrificing his own Son for our sins.[146] The Bible is not referring to an artificial passion that is fueled by a frantic quest to avoid painful self-reflection, nor a sinful passion based on lust. The Bible demands an authentic passion for good[147] that is fueled by gratitude for and awe of God's grace, mercy, and love, and is powered by the Holy Spirit.

However, this command is impossible to carry out consistently, especially during bad times,[148] if you've distanced yourself emotionally from people and places through self-medication and fear. [149]Contrast this with the numerous role models that scripture provides for us, from Abraham to Isaiah to Paul to Jesus Christ. As Christian author Philip Yancey aptly notes, "The giants of faith all had one thing in common: neither victory nor success, but passion."[150]

How about you? Malcolm Forbes said, "Men who never get carried away should be."[151] Can others see how passionate you are about sharing your faith in Jesus Christ? This is not a question of style—Christians range from wildly expressive to extraordinarily reserved—but of courageous, principled belief in action, which is enabled as we become less inhibited by self-medication and its diversions. This is true godly passion.

Creativity

Your *creativity* can remain unacknowledged or applied in the wrong directions when you self-medicate. Some of the most creative people I've known have regretfully applied their unique ability to fashion and craft toward all sorts of sinful pursuits and habits. Fortunately, however, history overflows with illustration after illustration of the awe-inspiring results when our God-given talent to create is joined with God's power of creation and change here on earth, that is, his Holy Spirit.

From the most beautiful fresco in a cathedral to the crayon-drawn family portrait your child proudly presents to you, or from the most awe-inspiring athletic achievement to the simplest expression of giving of one's self, godly creativity can touch others deeply and purely in ways that cannot be rationally explained otherwise.

We're all called to embrace creativity. Haddon Robinson from RBC Ministries reflects this when he says, "Love without deeds is useless, just as talent not demonstrated in creative ways is wasted. Both must be expressed or they are no better than a myth."[152] What if the fishermen called by Christ refused to consider that God could upgrade their skills into becoming fishers of men?[153] What if Andrew refused to consider that God could amplify the young boy's five loaves of bread and two small fish into dinner for five thousand people?[154] If you resist the Holy Spirit's guidance toward creation and change, how can God possibly instill more creativity within you?

Wholeness

Wholeness only comes as you see the depth of your brokenness first. Do you allow yourself to be vulnerable, to look within the deepest recesses of yourself? Said differently, do you ever allow yourself into a deeper intimacy within your *own* heart? If you cannot look at who and what you authentically are at this moment in your walk, then you are going to struggle in sharing God's love as effectively as he plans for you to.

Notice how Paul describes God's light within you. Just as a clay jar under stress reveals its contents as it breaks, God's light within you is exposed to the world as your body—described in scripture to be a "jar of clay"—suffers.[155] Although you may not feel that you can handle this stress at times, remember that Jesus says that his grace is sufficient for you during these troubling times.[156] In fact, his grace enables you to achieve greater levels of wholeness out of your broken state because you realize how astonishingly consistent his love is.

However, if you instead erect prideful, elaborate defenses to try to avoid facing the impact of past suffering, you're declaring that living in ignorance of your emotional holes is a higher priority than living out God's will for you. This is accompanied by a potentially huge impact on those close to you, not to mention the opportunity cost to your ministry. Do you want to be holy, or full of holes?

Holding someone else responsible for filling our emotional holes—for "making us happy"—is one of the more interesting and common defenses. This defense is most readily observable in troubled marriages, where some of the characteristics that attracted a spouse to his or her mate early in the relationship end up being seen as huge liabilities that lead to unfortunate consequences.

Why does this happen? Because we're often attracted to mates who tap into our unresolved issues. Let's look at a common example. A quiet woman with repressed anger is often attracted to an aggressive man who is openly comfortable with his emotions, despite other people seeing him as unpleasant and angry. For a while, the woman perceives that the impassive man makes her feel whole because she admires how comfortable he is with his feelings. As a result, she filters out any observations that don't fit with her perception of him, because feeling emotionally connected and personally "filled" is a more pressing need to her than having some "perfect gentleman" for a mate.

However, because only she can process her own issues, she eventually feels that emptiness creep back in. Because she has mistakenly been giving this man credit for filling in the holes caused by her unresolved anger that she refuses to discuss, she concludes that he must have changed. And as she starts looking at him more critically, dropping the filters that she previously viewed him through, she notices for the first time the things that he does that are distasteful. At this point, she will typically conclude that he must be the reason for her current feelings of emptiness, instead of realizing that she has been fooling herself by holding him responsible for something that he could never give her in the first place!

In the worst cases, where marriage and children are involved, divorce results, and the woman seeks someone else who makes her feel whole again ... and the cycle starts anew.

Can you see the need for personal wholeness? It is shocking sometimes to realize how much pain we cause each other from that which lies just out of sight of our conscious mind.

Unity

Let's look at the even bigger picture. Personal wholeness is not only for the benefit of ourselves and our current life companions. As we collectively experience wholeness, an even greater Christian union is achieved—*a spirit of unity.* As we become more authentic individually, the witness of our congregations grows collectively.[157] Here, a shared realization of the magnitude of God's greatness, grace, mercy, and love—and our total reliance on his saving power—leads us to bind together purposefully, humbly, and gently to carry out his divine plan through praise, worship, prayer, personal service, and sacrifice.[158]

Unity is Jesus's fundamental prayer for everyone[159]—including you and me, whom Jesus referred to as "future believers." Being united in his name will impact the world far more than any individual deeds done in his name. Scripture explains that our unity in him leads to a greater consistency and strength in our Christian walk, because we are less sidetracked, both individually and collectively, by the cunning and crafty temptations and teachings of Satan.[160]

Unity should lead to an acceptance of others that brings collective praise to God.[161] How can you personally help this to happen right now? Scripture teaches us that accepting each others' faults is one of the most fundamental things we can do,[162] which is one way we can love each other "without dissimulation." We're to offer forgiveness, patience, and prayer to build each other up, across all groups of people God has blessed us with—our spouse, children, parents, siblings, friends, church, community, and world—even if we can't always fully understand their viewpoint or motivations.

Empirical Results

In our research, many of the folks we've worked with have experienced fruitful and permanent life-changing breakthroughs after working through the four stages described in the previous chapter. Sometimes a breakthrough has occurred after following the cycle for the first time, and sometimes improvements have been more gradual, produced after repeating the cycle several times.

For example, when Harriet was able to recognize both her self-medication form (time martyr) and underlying root causes (parental absence during formative years) during her earliest work, she was able to process her sadness and immediately begin to set mature limits in her relationships.

On the other hand, while Simon was able to understand early in his first cycle how he was self-medicating through drugs and sex, he felt unable at that time to process his core issues. This caused him to trade up progressively to more socially acceptable forms of medication (namely work, and later ministry), instead of dealing with the root issues. After he was willing to address his real underlying root issue (sadness from a perceived lack of parental acceptance), he was finally able to throttle his rampant people-pleasing behavior. This allowed him to put God and his family first for the first time ever. This happened just in time, because his marriage was at the point of ending.

However, not everyone can give him- or herself permission to experience a breakthrough. Martha continues, as of this writing, to rationalize her pain away as a "cultural" issue, with ongoing pain and frustration resulting within both her and her family. Victor has, at least temporarily, given up believing that God can transform his marital pain into productivity, with a sad consequence of ongoing emotional separation.

Remember, only you can choose to adopt this process of authenticity, and follow through on it. *Please*, for the sake of your family and all those souls God will place along your path, make the courageous choice.

And do it ultimately for the right reason. As scripture commands, "whatever you do, do it all for the glory of God."[163] As your transforming relationships become a living witness, we will all be able to more clearly see God's glory at work.

Our world will truly be a better place for it.

Chapter Endnotes

[144] *Our Daily Bread* 50, no. 5 (1 August 2005).

[145] 2 Corinthians 4:16.

[146] Romans 12:11; Exodus 34:14 (NLT); Isaiah 9:6–7.

[147] Galatians 4:18.

[148] Romans 12:12.

[149] Revelations 3:15, 16.

[150] Yancey, Philip, *Reaching for the Invisible God* (Grand Rapids, MI: Zondervan, 2000), p. 178.

[151] Malcolm Forbes Quotes, http://www.brainyquote.com/quotes/authors/m/malcolm_forbes.html (accessed 4 September 2006).

[152] *Our Daily Bread* 50, no. 9 (26 December 2005).

[153] Matthew 4:18–20.

[154] John 6:5–13.

[155] 2 Corinthians 4:6–11.

[156] 2 Corinthians 12:9.

[157] 1 Corinthians 12:13.

[158] Ecclesiastes 4:8–12; Ephesians 4:2; Romans 12:1–5.

[159] John 17:20–23.

[160] Ephesians 4:13–16.

[161] Romans 15:5–6.

[162] Romans 15:7.

[163] 1 Corinthians 10:31.

Afterword
A Life-giving Opportunity

If you've been reading this book and you're not born anew in the Spirit of God, as Jesus Christ says you must be to inherit eternal life,[164] then you might be finding all this a bit fantastical, a bit mysterious, and even a bit far-fetched. How could this Holy Spirit of God, and how could this Jesus give you true and lasting inner peace and joy, and assure you of eternal life in heaven with him?

Because both are the ultimate gifts of God, the creator of everything—including you, me, and everyone else. He gives us the strength to make it through painful experiences and helps us better understand the others he places into our lives.

Even if you feel like you have messed up your life until now, and possibly the lives of others who have joined you on your path for a time, scripture offers irrefutable proof that God made the astounding decision to send his only Son to die for all of your sins. And mine. And everyone else's. Case closed. No penalty. No record.

All he asks is that you believe in his Son, Jesus Christ, who took the fall for you; that he died on the cross as a sin offering for you and me; that he rose from the dead to defeat evil, death, and sin.

Romans 10:9 states, "if you confess with your mouth, 'Jesus is Lord,' and believe in your heart that God raised him from the dead, you will be saved." Pray and accept Jesus Christ into your heart right now, and let his light shine fully within you so you can share it with others. And give up selfishly trying to carry those burdens by yourself. He'll help you shoulder them. After all, he's strong enough—he's God!

And if you started to believe long ago, but let the experiences he's tried to use to build your personal ministry drive you into self-medication and avoidance, then rededicate your life to him right now. And remember his unlimited power to pick you up and carry you through your struggles.

Such actions free us to fulfill his divine plan, fueled out of our gratitude for the eternal life we inherit from accepting Christ, not by forcing ourselves to try and fake feeling joy or being nice to someone else. We can be more creative and share unity and wholeness with his people as we serve them with true joy and passion.

Scripture says, "whoever sows sparingly will also reap sparingly, and whoever sows generously will also reap generously."[165] When your heart is in his hand, the heavy burdens are removed, and you will find it so much easier to "sow generously." You don't have to seek temporal happiness and peace through actions; your actions come naturally out of the joy and peace from the fruit he promises us through his Holy Spirit.[166]

It is easy to get off the correct path. As an illustration, many churches today contain many folks who are caught in an endless search, like a hamster on a wheel, seeking joy and peace through Christian activities. We don't find God by repeating the same deeds over and over. We find God's call that drives our deeds through faith and submission to him.

Christ said, "where your treasure is, there your heart will be also."[167] Let the Lord himself be your treasure, not the things in his creation. As your heart is increasingly open to his instruction, regardless of the circumstances, he will bless you more abundantly with greater opportunities to serve others and share the great joy, illumination, and peace that only he can provide.

This is the kind of world that God calls all of us to help him create. We're to share his light, unveiled, within our perishing world. Our passion, creativity, wholeness, and unity are desperately needed. God has blessed you with these capabilities through your unique gifts, but they come with a responsibility that self-medication and avoidance deny.

Let us all praise and worship the Almighty God and collectively step out in gratitude and love to compassionately serve his people more authentically today, starting with the most important people he's blessed your life with—your family.

Amen.

Chapter Endnotes

[164] John 3:3.

[165] 2 Corinthians 9:6.

[166] Galatians 5:22–23.

[167] Matthew 6:21; Luke 12:34.

APPENDIX

List of Feelings

This is a representative list of feelings that people experience from day to day.[168] How many of these do you recognize in scripture? For example, Jesus wept … [169]

Abandoned, Abused, Afraid, Alone, Angry, Annoyed, Anxious, Apologetic, Appreciative, Ashamed

Betrayed, Blamed, Bored

Caring, Cautious, Competitive, Condemned, Confused, Curious

Deceitful, Deceived, Defensive, Depressed, Disappointed, Disconnected, Disgusted

Embarrassed, Enraged, Enthusiastic, Excited

Fearful, Frustrated

Grateful, Grieving, Guilty

Happy, Helpful, Helpless, Hopeful, Hopeless, Hurt

Insecure, Insignificant, Inspired, Involved, Irritated

Jealous, Joyful

Lonely, Lost, Loved

Manipulated, Misunderstood

Nervous, Nurtured

Overwhelmed

Powerful, Powerless, Pressured

Regretful, Rejected, Relieved, Resentful

Sad, Suspicious, Sympathetic

Threatened, Tired, Trapped, Trustful

Unappreciated, Unimportant, Unloved, Used

Vengeful, Violated, Vulnerable

Weepy, Withdrawn, Worried

Endnotes

[168] Rodenbaugh, Marlene and Gary Gemmill. *Team Mirroring: Illusions and Realities of Team Dynamics and Development* (Doyletown, PA: HANDLEY Group, 2004); David Ferguson and Don McMinn. *Emotional Fitness: Developing a Wholesome Heart.* (Irving, TX: Intimacy Press, 2003).

[169] John 11:35.

Suggested Readings and Select Bibliography

The Holy Bible (any translation).

Scripture in this book taken from The Holy Bible, New International Version (copyright 1973, 1978, 1984 by International Bible Society); The Promise Keepers Men's Study Bible, King James Version (Grand Rapids, MI: Zondervan, 1997); and The Holy Bible, New Living Translation (Wheaton, IL: Tyndale House Publishers, Inc., 1996).

Argyris, Chris. *Overcoming Organizational Defenses: Facilitating Organizational Learning.* Needham Heights, MA: Allyn and Bacon, 1990.

Eldredge, John. *Wild at Heart: Discovering the Secret of a Man's Soul.* Nashville, TN: Thomas Nelson, 2001.

Ferguson, David and Don McMinn. *Emotional Fitness: Developing a Wholesome Heart.* Irving, TX: Intimacy Press, 2003.

Gemmill, Gary. "Leadership in the Shadow of 9/11." *Ephemera* 2, no. 1 (2002): 53–60.

"The Dynamics of Scapegoating in Small Groups." *Small Group Behavior* 20, no. 4 (1989): 406–418.

Gemmill, Gary and Michael Elmes. "Mirror, Mask and Shadow: Psychodynamics Aspects of Intergroup Relationships." *Journal of Management Inquiry* 2, no. 1 (1993).

"The Psychodynamics of Group Mindlessness and Dissent in Small Groups." *Small Group Research* 21, no. 2 (1990): 28–44.

Gemmill, Gary and George Kraus. "Dynamics of Covert Role Analysis: Small Groups." *Small Group Behavior* 19, no. 3 (1988): 299–311.

Goleman, Daniel. *Emotional Intelligence: Why it can matter more than IQ.* New York: Bantam, 1997.

Life Application Bible, New International Version edition. Grand Rapids, MI: Zondervan, 1991.

Loritts, Jr., Crawford W. *Make It Home Before Dark: God's Call to Holiness in Our Walk with him.* Chicago: Moody Press, 2000.

McGee, Robert S. *The Search for Significance.* Nashville, TX: W Publishing Group, 2003.

Rodenbaugh, Marlene and Gary Gemmill. *Team Mirroring: Illusions and Realities of Team Dynamics and Development.* Doylestown, PA: HANDLEY Group, 2004.

Romanowski, William. *Eyes Wide Open.* Grand Rapids, MI: Brazos Press, 2001.

Yancey, Philip. *Reaching for the Invisible God.* Grand Rapids, MI: Zondervan, 2000.

About the Author

Bob Kalka has more than sixteen years of experience and research in the theory and psychodynamics of groups, having worked under the tutelage of Dr. Gary Gemmill, one of the world's prominent published experts in this area. Bob is president and cofounder of Gemmill, Kalka and Associates (www.gemka.org), a Christian organization dedicated to helping people remove the hidden barriers to living more authentically. He is also a frequent international lecturer on the intersection of business psychodynamics and information technology at a Fortune 10 corporation.

Bob holds an MBA in Organizational Change and Development from Syracuse University in Syracuse, New York; a Bachelor of Science Degree in Computer Science with an emphasis on Philosophy from the Rochester Institute of Technology in Rochester, New York; and a Certificate in Strategic Marketing Planning from the Indiana University Graduate School of Business in Bloomington, Indiana. He lives in central Texas with his wife, Kelly, and their children, Jonathan and Lauren.

978-0-595-42043-8
0-595-42043-5

9 780595 420438